My Endearing Appalachia

Memoirs of Southern West Virginia Coalfield Life

Phylenia French

International Standard Book Number 0-87012-944-9
Library of Congress Control Number 2023900867
Printed in the United States of America
Copyright © 2023 by Phylenia French
Christiansburg, VA
All Rights Reserved
2023

McClain Printing Company
Parsons, WV
www.mcclainprinting.com
2023

Table of Contents

1. Where My Family Legacy Began   1
2. The Birth of the Coal Camp Communities   8
3. The Communities of My Childhood   11
4. Carswell   11
5. Bottom Creek   13
6. Maitland   19
7. Lives Interrupted   29
8. Home and Drugstore Remedies Remembered   35
9. Signs of the Times and Activities on the Homefront   40
10. Back Porch Friends, Pin Curls, and Coalfield Life   52
11. That's Entertainment!   55
12. School Days   65
13. Watching for Momaw and Popaw   77
14. Saturday Night: Kinfolks, Cement Fudge and Burnt Popcorn Kernels   78
15. Summer Vacations   81
16. More Gems from a Childhood Treasury   86
17. Church Goin' and the Inception of Assembly of God Church   91
18. Tribute to Momma   95
19. Tribute to Daddy   102
20. Closing Remarks   105

My Endearing Appalachia
Memoirs of Southern West Virginia Coalfield Life

We were in West Virginia to spend some time at my childhood homeplace on a very early spring day. The moment I set my feet on the mountain dirt, I began to look around the playground of my childhood. Blooms of white and pink joined the deep purple of the wild Violet to usher in springtime. Sprouts of Mayapple, Ferns and a fresh growth of Green Briers were twining their way through the dirt. That is the mystery and beauty of a rugged mountain where the tiniest of flowers emerged with amazing strength through the tough briers, rocks, and dirt. These little beauties did not give up their places in my mountains. They were determined to press through and rise to the surface and bloom. Yes, their exhibits reminded me of the value of my childhood experiences in my mountain home.

As I walked through the overgrowth of thorny branches and made wider steps over small streams of water that were flowing from the mountain, I began to rewind some of the memories that I have stored in my heart and soul. I was looking for the path that led us over the hill, the path over which we made our way to school; and that led us by Sam and Dorothea's house.

Once we reached the top of the hill, after making our way over the steep gullies that had been carved out over time, the mountain breezes produced an exhilaration filled with memories.

As I stood there with my hubby, the early spring sunshine wrapped me in a sentimental and warming drape of nostalgia, like a downy soft comforter on a chilly morning. That moment was filled with pictures from the past, rapidly re-winding to a time over sixty years ago.

Several trains passed through the community while we were up there on the mountain and the haunting echo of the train whistle and the rumbling of the massive tons of metal against the tracks, turned the clock back to the years of my childhood. If we walked through the camp going home after school, we stopped at the tracks to wait as trains passed before we made our ascent to the mountain. When the steam engine began to belch out gigantic, billowing, black smoke clouds, we knew not to look upward because the cinders from the clouds would drop in our eyes and our hair. We kids were the only ones who lived on that hillside, and we had paths carved from years of footprints for school days and summertime berry picking. While walking around the property, and when that train whistle began, I was suddenly transported to a school day and found myself emerging at the top of the hill and walking around to the "back" of my house to find Momma hanging clothes on the line and at another time, I "saw" her on the porch as she yelled at my brother and his friend to "Come down off that cliff, right now!" Nearby I saw the coal box that stored our winter supply and a stack of rough wood, with the chopping block and the axe leaning against the building.

That spring visit evoked memories as I wished I had brought something tangible from my childhood home. So, I began to write.

A picture of a small girl sitting beside the porch steps, in the yard that was sparsely covered with the green of crab grass over a rocky surface embedded with slack from the coal that was carried in for the heating and cook stoves. It didn't matter that the wooden walkway led straight to the steps and was a risk of intrusion on her private dreams. It was easy to shut off everything around her while she painted her pictures in the frame of her fantasies.

She drew aside, just to sit there, quietly engrossed with the wish book known as a Sears, Roebuck catalog. Thumbing through the slick pages with photos of elegantly dressed brides in flowing lengths of white lace, stirred her imagination that one day, she would be the bride. Why, even the casual attire of pedal pushers and sleeveless blouses had a sophistication that impressed her young mind. She looked with deepest admiration at the images of the women modeling the clothing and began to travel into the future, planning her wardrobe and destinations. She had never traveled to faraway places. Her images of the future were framed in her fantasies. Little did she know that the actual events and places she enjoyed would be the fuel that kept a little girl's imagination flickering. These moments alone activated her dreams of what she would have when she grew up. Interestingly, her fantasies were set within the boundaries of her present conditions and the limited knowledge of a small child. Those dreams of "when I grow up", so she thought, would include the primitive wood and coal fired stoves, the wringer washing machine and the path to the outhouse. Who knew? "Yes, who knew!" how modern advances would change our daily life. Those chores were assigned according to gender of the children in the family, and she envisioned that her children would be a boy and a girl, and they would have their role specific place in her life.

Acknowledgments

This book is dedicated to our children, Timothy and Teresa, our granddaughter, Britni, and my husband, Buddy.

Thank you, Norma and Julia, for sharing your photos of Superior-Maitland May Day Festival.

Introduction

    Black lung had claimed another life! Despite the sentence pronounced upon them, the men who entered the mines for a livelihood developed a strong devotion and love for the land and the mountains where veins of black gold promised prosperity. The risk was clear yet there was money to be made through the labor of sweat and tears to support a family. As I recount my life in the coalfields, I remember that coal was not the only natural resource we depended upon for a livelihood. You will notice we took advantage of nature's bounty in other ways as well. With Appalachian roots from which I grew, my life as a child in the coalfields conferred upon me responsibility and as a result, I learned the art of creativity and resourcefulness. Both my work and play revolved around nature, the perfect learning environment.

    I want to invite you to peer over my shoulders as I paint for you a picture of bygone days in the coalfields of southern West Virginia.

    The backdrop of my canvas will be the mountains and the rock cliff that stood behind my house. I will draw that picture with a wider brush. Those wide brush strokes will show you that beside my house there is a huge water tank that supplies the community. And there is a path carved out on the side of the hill where we made our way to a vegetable garden annually. That path served a dual purpose as we traveled to the mountains as children to explore from daylight 'til dark when weather permitted. For the continuation of my story, I will fill in my canvas with softer bristles at times of good and bad, but with well-defined brush strokes that paint a portrait of the strength of the people in the coal camps as well as the children who stand against tragedies that encroach upon life's everyday routine.

I want you to see, feel, hear, and touch the very presence of family life in the coalfields when we were children.

The wife of the coal miner was the glue that held the home environment together and kept the domestic wheels turning and running smoothly while her husband earned the pay that kept groceries on the table. The coal miner who arrived home at the end of his shift, was exhausted and needed the comfort and love that family can give.

Monday in the coal camp was the day set aside for laundry. As we approach wash day in the mountains, I want you to hear the swishing and grinding of the Maytag washer's agitator and smell the Fleecy white bleach and Tide detergent. Get a whiff of the Octagon laundry soap as it is rubbed into the stains of clothing across an old washboard (or as some called it a (warshboard).

See the laundry strung out on the clothesline, clothing displayed in groups, towels, sheets, shirts, pants, undergarments, artfully arranged and dried awaiting removal to the house where some items will be dunked in a starchy bath that contained Satina, for pressing into a smooth finish.

I want you to feel the heat from the red embers glowing in the Warm Morning stove in the living room and smell the ashes being pulled from under the grate in the old Majestic cook stove in the kitchen. We had to keep the ashes out so the fire could breathe and raise the oven temperature. That was necessary for the duration of meal preparations which included breads. Children were taught hard work and joined in the effort of running a household. Usually, chores were assigned according to gender in the era in which I lived in the coal camps. At least it "seemed" to be that way. I, myself, often would swing an axe and chop wood and many times have filled a bucket and carried in coal from outside.

Hard work. Hard times. Good times. And happy times. Heartwarming and heartbreaking experiences. In all these places, each family member dealt with individual responses to them, yet we needed each other.

I am so thankful that my mother was there for me in my formative years. And I believe that my simple upbringing, along with shared responsibility in my mountain home were part of the maturing process for my future adult life.

Where My Family Legacy Began

Daddy was born in a rustic, log farmhouse in Mt. Airy, North Carolina, delivered by a midwife named Amanda Gerard, a housekeeper who lived in nearby Cana, Virginia. He grew up there until he was twenty years old. His time in North Carolina presented a different social landscape. Popaw Snow made moonshine in the back woods of North Carolina. He paid some fines in the process. And there was an incident with one of my relatives, JR, who was sent to take a lunch to a particular spot in the woods where a still was actively brewing some 'shine. JR, with broken leg, went down to where the still was located and he encountered the law who had arrived to destroy the still. Those who were operating the still, ran and got away, but JR could not run due to his broken leg. Consequently, he was fined. So, he decided to build his own still to make enough money to pay the fine. Well, his efforts resulted in a still that blew up, sending mushroom clouds rising out of the treetops. The smoke was seen from the kitchen window of one of my aunts who lived in the area. I was told by another relative that JR grew a beard and laid low for the duration of that summer. I don't know if he abandoned the idea of ever making 'shine again. I lost track of him many years ago.

Uncle Edgar, Daddy at three years old, and Aunt Etta, in North Carolina.

Long before this incident with JR, according to a receipt dated March 9, 1914, Popaw Snow had a fine of fifty dollars imposed on him in Hillsville Virginia at the Carroll County courthouse, but the reason is not noted. We think it was probably related to his involvement with moonshine.

Daddy arrived in Coalwood, West Virginia in 1939 to begin work at the Carter Coal Company, which later became Olga Coal Company.

Uncle Ernest and Aunt Pearl in Coalwood WV. Ca. 1920s. Below is Olga Coal company tipple.

Olga Coal Company. Daddy began work there in 1939, when it was called Carter Coal.

He worked first as a bone picker (the process of separating coal from slate as it came through a conveyor), making four dollars and forty-six cents a day. Later he became a motorman and brakeman on the motorcars that carried the men deep inside the mines. Eventually he became a skilled welder, the vocation he practiced until retirement.

Momma was born in Baileysville, West Virginia where Popaw worked in the mines during a time when mules were used to pull the coal cars inside to be loaded. I don't know how long Popaw worked there, but when Momma was six months old, in 1924, Hugh Andrew and Susie Baker, decided to move from there. They packed their belongings including some furniture and boarded a train for Coalwood. When they settled in Coalwood, Popaw was hired to be custodian at the doctor's office and to keep the fires going for heating businesses in town. Popaw contracted silicosis from exposure to the environment in which he worked.

    They set up housekeeping in the section known as Frog Level. That was the scene of Momma's childhood activity. She said many of the kids in the community enjoyed playing around the ball field. As I quizzed her about her life in Coalwood, she recounted a notable incident: Momma was older by now and as Momaw and Popaw tended a garden on the hillside near the ball field, Momma was responsible for babysitting her younger brother, Jack. His curiosity led him to climb the bleacher stairs toward the roof where he took a fall that frightened Momma out of her wits! Amazingly, there were no serious injuries to her brother, and she escaped what might have been severe disciplinary action. Coal camp ball games were a welcomed summertime sport, but she told me that some people could not afford the price of a ticket for admission, so many would bring blankets and spread them on the ground above the field and observe from the hillside free of charge.

    When she was a teenager, she found a way to earn some personal money, so she offered to iron for women in the neighborhood and Pearl Snow was one of those women. For posterity, I asked Momma exactly how she and Daddy met in Coalwood considering that he was from another state. Momma told me that she spotted Daddy from the kitchen window where she stood ironing clothes for her future sister in-law, Pearl. Pearl was married to my daddy's brother, Ernest, who was originally from North Carolina, but had moved to Coalwood.

Aunt Pearl informed my mother that she had told her brother in-law about a girl she wanted him to meet. Now, he never cared for red hair, so he asked, "Does she have red hair?" My aunt replied with a smile in her voice, "Yes, as a matter of fact she does, it's auburn red." So, on this occasion, as Momma continued ironing, Daddy stepped up on the porch and walked into the house and into the life of my auburn-haired momma. Further delving into the past, I learned that their courtship included Saturday night dates, sitting on the porch swing while accompanied by the Grand Ole Opry on radio. I also learned that one of Daddy's favorite songs was Sunrise Serenade by the Glenn Miller orchestra. He enjoyed the big band sounds of the forties.

I guess the auburn hair and the musical radio programs proved to be sweet harmony in the romance that led to their wedding day when Momma was not quite seventeen. I asked Momma if she was jealous of Daddy when they were dating and she confessed that she had been. Seems there was a young girl named Rosalie that tried to compete for Daddy's attention as they strolled through the neighborhood. Momma was able to keep her composure during those times of courtship so that kept things in order. Momma's role in our family influenced me greatly. Daddy was more of an authoritarian when it came to parenting.

Trapped in the clutches of modern technology demands forward progress. So, I now pause from time to time and draw from an inner well of memories of my youthful experiences in my mountain home. It is then that I can once again, surround myself with the warmth of extended family, friends, and neighbors.

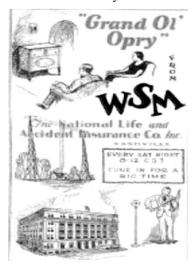

The coalfield lifestyle was like no other as the coal barons came and opened mines all over the state of West Virginia. For every family who had residence there in those communities, they shared familiarity of lifestyles that included shopping and worship and children's school years strengthened friendships. And the miners dressed alike wearing blue or gray work clothes, hard hats and safety toe shoes.

At Aunt Ethel's house in North Carolina.
Aunt Ethel, Daddy, Momma, Teddy in front.

Log house similar to the one in which Daddy was born

Tobacco barn

Momaw and Popaw Snow

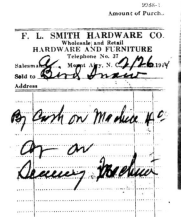

Hardware Store

Momaw Snow standing by car parked near tobacco barn

STATE OF NORTH CAROLINA,
Surry County.
1919 DOG LICENSE
This is to certify that ~~Bird Byrd~~
has paid $1.00 privilege tax for keeping a dog or bitch, as required by law.
Dated at Dobson, N. C., ...1919
............Sheriff.

B No. 3781
Series H

$50.00

County (or City) of *Carroll* Va.
Hillsville, Va. *Mar. 9* 1914
This is to Certify, That *Bird Snow*
has paid me **FIFTY DOLLARS**, being the amount of a fine imposed according to law upon _____

Countersigned by
C. Lee Moore
Auditor of Public Accounts

Clerk (or Justice)

Stewarts Creek Township, *Sept 3* 1904
RECEIVED OF *Bird Snow*
his Taxes for the year 1903, as follows:
For State Tax, - - - $ .57
" County Tax, - - - 2.10
" Poll Tax, - - - ____
$ 2.88
............Sheriff.
$ _____ J. H. East ....D. S.

SURRY COUNTY, N. C.
No. 10695
Stewarts Creek Township *17* 1925

Received of *Bird Byrd*
taxes for 1925 as follows:
Poll Tax - - - $ 2.59
General School 53c - - 6.02
County 12c - - - 1.36
Int. on Bonds 25c - - 2.83
Roads 14c - - - 1.59
Bridge 3c - - - .34
Special Bond 3c - - .34
Dog Tax - - - .20
Total - - - $ 17.05

Total Valuation Discount—Penalty, $ .27
$ 1132   17.32
............Sheriff

The Birth of the Coal Camp Communities

Where the rich veins of black gold were being mined from the mountains, the mine owners established communities or coal "camps" for their employees. Houses were either cottage-type, or what we called double houses (duplex). There were clubhouses built mainly for single men. The superintendent's house always sat up on a hill above the camp, seemingly, as a symbol of his position with the company.

The owner of the mines or Coal Company made other provisions for the workers (in addition to the houses). With the arrival of immigrants of diverse ethnicities, the development of the community considered with respect, the varied houses of worship accordingly, which would include Orthodoxy, Catholics, Protestants and Jewish. There was a beautiful blend in communities of workers from Russia, Hungary, Poland, Greece, Italy, just to name several. Not only were we introduced to traditions of worship, but it included the marvelous introduction to cooking styles. The immigrants brought with them expert skills which they invested in the building of a community as iron workers, stone masons, and carpenters. Evidence remains today of those skills when one visits a location where once thriving communities existed.

The building of the community also included a grocery store, drugstore, schools, a medical doctor's office, theaters, and recreational facilities that included bowling alleys and dance halls. There were also baseball teams that the company organized and proved to be extremely popular through the years.

The Coal Companies hired a physician for the employees and required each miner to pay a monthly sum of around five dollars to have access to health care. When one had to go to the company doctor, following an examination, the doctor would then act as pharmacist by counting out pills and placing them in a small, brown envelope and writing instructions for use in long hand. The most prescribed medicine I remember was a small, black pill given for croup. It had a peculiar smell but was highly effective in results. We called them, simply, croup pills. A shot of penicillin was a frequent and dreaded treatment during those days of company doctors.

The pattern for the design of coal camps served every aspect of daily life and provided convenient access to all the needed services and recreations. There also were hospitals established nearby.

I feel fortunate that my parents raised me in my mountain home and that I had the opportunity to share my education with the same friends from first grade through the twelfth and to join in civic organizations for Girl and Boy Scouts. Adults were members of Fraternal organizations like the Odd Fellows, Masons and women joined the International Association of the Rebekah lodge as well as women's ministries in their preferred churches.

These organizations with closely knit friendships, provided a social outlet for the men and women. And they scheduled annual picnic events for the whole family. I was invited to go with my then boyfriend's family to a fish fry picnic at Panther State Park. He came with his parents to my house in a 1952 Ford pickup truck, and he and I rode in the back of the truck to the event, enjoying the scenic, winding roads as we traveled. The coal company employees formed baseball teams for the men and bowling leagues were enjoyed as well.

Carswell Company Store

Carswell Mine

Kimball 1940

Peerless Company Store
courtesy of ERCA

The Communities of My Childhood

King section of Carswell, my birthplace.

Carswell, where our baby brother was born.

Carswell

I was born in a section of Carswell called King. We were not there long before we moved "farther up in the holler." It was there that our baby brother, Jackie was born. Momma went into labor and Momaw called the family doctor in. Once that was done, she corralled us kids and said, before the doctor had arrived, "Come on now, get on up the stairs and stay there!" We got a quick glimpse through the window of the doctor carrying his black medical bag as he was coming into the house, but it wasn't long before Momaw, like a traffic cop on duty was rushing us out of the living room and up the stairs.

Once we were there, our curiosity got the better of us and we went over to a floor vent to try to see what was going on downstairs but to no avail. I suppose our young minds thought, "well if I'm not supposed to see what's going on, then I must "need" to see what the excitement was about. Amazing what stands out in our memory from a young age and how it compares to where we are today in society where whole families get invited in to witness a birth.

I do not recall our length of stay in that house, but we eventually moved to another camp, called Bottom Creek.

Bottom Creek today. A lone church sits near where our house sat over sixty years ago.

Bottom Creek ca.1920s. Our house was about halfway up this road. This is where jumping rope caused my injury to my forehead. It was in the early 1950s.

Bottom Creek

From Bottom Creek, we walked to Vivian where our elementary school year began. We crossed railroad tracks, walking by the company store and then on to the schoolhouse. Ms. Rayburn was my teacher for the time spent there. I remember that we were grouped at tables rather than individual desks. Because we moved soon after I began first grade, I can't recall other physical arrangements of the classroom and I did not get to establish friendships.

The need for miners depended on the demand for coal from the Coal Company that was in operation at that time. Men could move from camp to camp in order to support their families. This is the reason my family made several moves within the coal camps.

Though I was quite young when we lived in Bottom Creek, I vividly recall one of our neighbors; a Hungarian man named John, who had only one arm. As a result, when we spoke of him, we addressed him as "One Armed John". Obviously, today this would be forbidden, but at that time, we used certain phrases to refer to someone, just to identify a specific person, not to be critical or demeaning. My memory of this man, John, seems to be a reflection only of his solitary life because I do not remember his mingling much with the people of the camp, consequently we did not learn much about his family. Sifting through my memory, I see a lone, short man topped off with a black beret that crowned his face of orange peel skin and a prominent, bulbous nose. His long-sleeved shirts always had one arm folded in half and pinned to his shoulder.

I remember watching the ice truck pull up in front of his house and the driver, using large tongs, lifted out a gigantic cube of ice and carried it to his back porch, where he placed it in the bottom of a wooden ice box.

I had a childhood friend tell me that she used to work for this man cleaning his house and she recalled that she was sent to borrow sugar from him for her mother to make a pie.

The fact that John was our neighbor allowed me to observe differences in others which I might otherwise have missed. I treasure the knowledge I gained as we lived in different camps early in my life.

At five years old, I felt I had mastered the ability to jump rope. So, seeking a challenge, I thought it would be interesting to see if I could run and jump rope at the same time. Well, away I went, skipping down the road until I fell flat on my face in the middle of the asphalt road and lay open a nasty gash in my forehead! I was scared for some strange reason, to go home to be checked, so I ran under Mrs. Trump's porch, who, when she saw my plight, wiped my bloody face and took me by the hand and walked me home with blood streaming down my face. My mother was so hysterical, she jumped the fence to go across the road and ask someone to drive me to the company doctor. We must not have owned a car at that time and because the tipple where my dad worked was in walking distance of our house it must not have been necessary. My uncle's brother-in-law drove me to the doctor and my office visit required extended time because the gash in my forehead demanded sutures.

When it came time to have the stitches removed from my head, I remember Daddy walking me down the road, barefooted, across the railroad tracks, leaving my footprints in the coal slack from the tipple, and up a hill to Doc Ficken's office which was situated in a large, rambling house. Daddy picked me up, coal black feet bottoms on display and set me on the exam table where Doc Ficken would remove the stitches and pronounce me healed. Daddy and I left the doctor's office with me bearing the reward of one lollipop for cooperating.

Shortly into the school year at Vivian elementary, Daddy moved us to Maitland and I completed my first grade there.

Koppers Coal Company. Our house set on the mountainside above the mine.

Koppers Company Store, Maitland, WV. Our house is behind the store.

Miner's cap and light

Dinner bucket

Maitland sign

Welch, WV, where my Momma shopped every two weeks.

Maitland Cliff house spot

Momma and me, 1961

Handmade swing, held together with wooden pegs

WATSON LANDS - McDOWELL COUNTY
Farm Lease dated January 1, 1955, to Parlie I. Snow.

Welch, West Virginia, January 10, 1955.

Mr. Clyde V. Bailey, Land Agent:

I hand you herewith executed counterparts of lease dated January 1, 1955, to Parlie I. Snow which is a new lease on the subject lands. The House was formerly House No. 138 in Maitland Camp. This lease was made upon the recommendation of Darrell B. Dunn, Assistant Land Agent, to afford us protection in regard to Camp supply water tanks and to relieve us of maintenance on this house apart from the main Camp.

The lease has been explained to the Lessee and he accepts same with full knowledge of its contents; he agrees to abide by all the terms and covenants of the lease, to render all service possible in the prevention and suppression of forest fires and to notify promptly of any acts of any one which might be against the interests of Lessor.

Improvements:

2 acres cleared land
4-room, one-story boxed house in bad condition
1 1-place garage
2 small outbuildings
1 outside toilet
Camp water
Electricity

C. E. McGuyer

P.O.Address: Box 65
Superior, W. Va.

#M—3-55—S.

Date of Lease Jan. 1, 1955 Term One Year Lessee Parlie I. Snow
Acreage 2 On Waters of Elkhorn Creek Tract Watson Lands
Rental $40.00 Rent Begins Jan. 1, 1955 Payable Jan. 1 annually in advance. McDowell County

DATE OF PAYMENT			AMOUNT		PAID TO			REMARKS F-748
Year	Month	Day	Dollars	Cents	Year	Month	Day	
1955	Apr.	30	4	11	1956	Jan.	1	Supersedes lease dated to
1956	Feb.	2	36	00		an acct.		
1956	May	11	40	00	1957	Jan.	1	
1957	May	10	40	00	1958	Jan.	1	
1958	June	6	40	00	1959	"	1	

Witness the following signatures and seals as of the date hereof.
Executed in Triplicate.

POCAHONTAS LAND CORPORATION,
By ....(Seal)
Agent.
Parlie I. Snow (Seal)

State of West Virginia } to wit:
County of McDowell

I, C. E. McGuyer, a Notary Public of said County, do certify that Parlie I. Snow, whose name is signed to the writing above, dated January 1, 19 55, has this day acknowledged the same before me in my said County.

Given under my hand this 10 day of January, 19 55.

My commission expires February 17, 1964. C. E. McGuyer
Notary Public.

Bottom Creek Coal and Coke Company
courtesy ERCA

Maitland

Maitland is where I spent most of my childhood. We were about two miles from Welch. From Route 52, a bridge crosses Elkhorn Creek and leads into the camp. There was an African American church at the end of the bridge and during summertime meetings when the door was left ajar, we were blessed with beautiful distant sounds of singing and rejoicing. There is a sign on the utility pole in this picture and an arrow on it points left to the road that leads to the airport on Belcher Mountain. It was a small airport and occasionally Daddy would drive us up there to watch the planes land or take off. My little brother Teddy was standing at the fence

Maitland Camp ca. 1948

watching a plane get ready for take off and when the engine started, he jumped and ran as fast as his feet would carry him. Momma and Daddy got a big laugh out of that event.

The other sounds that filled the air at our homeplace came from the ribbons of steel as the steam engine's massive tons of metal vibrated against the tracks and the haunting sound of its whistle echoed from the mountains. That sound evokes a romantic longing in the soul to return to the mountain of my childhood.

Recently, I received the lease agreement that Daddy had signed to take possession of the house and property. I asked someone who works for the Land company (which is still in operation today), if he would look in their historic files and locate my daddy's name and find the papers. He did and provided me with the copy, first dated in 1953. Stipulations were clearly defined on that deed. The land company gave permission for him to make limited additions to a house that had been disassembled in the camp and brought up on the mountain to be reassembled. Daddy built a couple of room additions. The deed noted how much could be allotted to gardening and keeping animals as well. We did not have a bathroom inside, but Daddy built a shower room with a concrete floor and built-in shelves and sink. He added marbles in the floor near the drain. A unique touch to his work.

Once we moved in and with each season's change, came new explorations and opportunities to add to our memories, which were like filling a refreshing well from which to draw and be energized. Reminiscing about that led me to remember many other details.

This property where my childhood home sat many years ago is the palette from which I paint my stories and reflections etched in my mind. And this is where significant steps were carved as we covered every inch of dirt for our times of play and explorations and unleashing our curiosities with youthful abandon. One landmark spot on the yard was where a large rock jutted from the earth and the magnificently fragrant Locust tree stood in full white, bloom in summer. And it was far enough from the house to "feel" private. My siblings and I could, as young children, whisper with confidence to each other if we had a secret meeting. I drew in my mind the wooden walkway that led to the porch, where it met the steps.

In reading that lease agreement, some parts in handwriting and some in old fashioned type print, kept the scenes of my childhood vividly on parade through my mind and created a heartwarming nostalgia around me. And I wondered what Daddy would have been feeling as he put his signature on that paper. There had to be a sense of relief knowing he had secured a place for his family as well as a place to garden to provide food for us.

As I continued reading the stipulations and noting the signatures of the representatives of the coal company, memories kept surfacing. They were unending with every word, drawing yet another picture of our homeplace.

A brick and wood post office building was located next to the railroad track. A family occupied part of the building. I remember seeing the heavy, canvas, mail bags being tossed from the train to the yard of the post office as the train raced by.

We walked through the camp on our return home from school sometimes and consequently we were apt to encounter an approaching train on the tracks we crossed to make our way up the hill to our house. We stood back a safe distance and waited as the train passed with heavy, black, sulfuric smoke billowing from its stack. We knew not to look upward as the train sped by because the shower of cinders raining down upon our scalp could fill our eyes as well.

Our common method of going places required walking. In the mountains, on a hillside, where paths were carved by footsteps making their way to school each day. If we walked through the back door, we were "walking the back way" to school and it led to a foot bridge over Elkhorn creek, then through a tunnel underneath the highway that exited at the steps that led us up to the schoolhouse door.

On that hill is where our house sat in front of the cliff and the mountains behind that cliff were my classroom... Rhododendrons bloomed in summer and wildflowers in colors of white and crimson and orange, were on display as I carried my biscuit and jelly and Mason jar filled with Kool-Aid to my favorite picnic spot. Toad stools happily occupied the dark green moss that grew at the base of trees adding to the beauty of the woods. Then I sat down under the Rhododendron and let my imagination create the travel plan for where I would go next…whether in the present or in the future. It was a matter of imagination as to where I mapped out the journey. And as I made my way out of the mountains, I would search for the strongest grapevine along the way, yanking as hard as I could to test for safety, and spend some time swinging in the air for a few minutes of excitement to close out my trip to my secret spot. We had a myriad of ways of entertaining ourselves as we roamed about our mountain home; even the Sears, Roebuck catalog was a great source of entertainment and mental stimulus for the childlike imagination. I have always said, "If you can read, you can travel anywhere you want to go." If those mountains could just whisper about the occasions we wandered there; if they could record the number of footsteps we made as we picked abundant blackberries in the summer...What would these majestic peaks say to our soul?

And the road that led to our house on the side of the mountain is the same road we walked down to make our way to the school bus stop each morning during high school. We created a shortcut walking by Sam and Dorothea's house, to the main road through the camp that crossed the railroad tracks and led to the bridge we crossed where our bus would stop for us.

In Maitland, our closest neighbors and very dear friends were Sam and Dorothea, a Black couple. They were like family to us. Their dwelling was a three room, roughly built, wooden structure which sat against a dirt hill, with a sloping front yard and a path leading to the porch steps. It was heated by coal stoves. And, of course, there was the infamous outhouse.

We had a foot path about halfway down our road that we followed, and the path crossed a road used by trucks hauling red dog (cinders and waste) from the mine. I remember that the bank of the uke road was embedded with gray, clay dirt which was fun for sculpting and squishing and momentary enjoyment along the path. That path took us through Sam and Dorothea's property.

My most vivid recollections of these folks are very warm and family oriented. Sam, a tall, stout individual with a gentle demeanor worked for a local man who owned a small "punch" mine. I can clearly remember the kneepads he wore for his work in helping to dig the low coal from inside the mountains. On occasional weekends, Sam would decide to come up on a Saturday afternoon with checkerboard in hand, to see Daddy and challenge him to a game of checkers. Sitting down to a game of checkers was a favorite pastime for Daddy and Sam. Sometimes they shared a drink together during the game. Sam was the champion of all checker players and I do not believe Daddy ever won a game!

And Dorothea, a short, pudgy woman, kept her hair in short braids pinned close to her scalp. Very rarely, she would visit a beautician to have her hair straightened and set in waves, which she said was done with a hot iron. Through the wide gaps between her teeth, you could detect stains from the Big G snuff she packed inside her cheek. Dorothea was a free-spirited individual. And we loved to tell her funny stories because her whole body quaked as she threw her head back and shrieked with laughter.

There was a compassionate side to Sam and Dorothea as well. They would rally for us when family members could not. When my brother was involved in a life-threatening car accident, my mom and dad were called to the hospital at one o'clock in the morning and Dorothea willingly came to sit with us while our parents drove the forty-five miles trip.

Because they had no children, they treated my siblings and me as if we were their very own. Granted, segregation was a dishonorable thing in our country for too many years, but during those days, I had no knowledge of what segregation was. I know my parents did not speak ill of people of different backgrounds and I never heard anything of prejudices.

Even though their house was only a three-room dwelling, they accommodated two boarders, named James "Hamp" Hamilton and Alexander "Zan" Joyce. They were friendly men and they didn't have extended families. But Zan was the only one who climbed the hill to come visit at our house. Zan's clothing was overalls and flannel shirts most of the time and they were very worn, as were his shoes that had holes in the sides. He kept a can of Prince Albert cigarette tobacco in his shirt pocket and a package of rolling papers. He would roll and light a cigarette while sitting in the swing and enjoy watching traffic on Route 52 just to pass the time.

From our house on the side of the mountain we had a panoramic view of the camp so that may be the reason he visited. If Daddy ever needed his help with anything, he answered the call. In cold weather if he was at our house, and we needed to bring in a bucket of coal, he would volunteer his help.

On July 4th holidays, Sam and Dorothea treated us very generously to summer coolers like watermelon, ice cream and pop. In those days, money earned by the miners was used for only the bare necessities, so soda pop or ice cream was truly a welcomed luxury.

Socializing with our black friends was a rewarding experience, for we learned much about their ethnic background as a result. One significant memory I have of

Dorothea's own resourcefulness involved her biscuit making. After heating an empty, Carnation milk can a few minutes on top of the cook stove, she would use a knife to knock the top off creating an excellent, biscuit cutter.

Dorothea's cooking was delicious too! In her coal-fired, antique cook stove, she made egg custard pies and biscuits that would rival any delicatessen. She made sausage patties for supper sometimes and she would add onion and an egg with breadcrumbs and when those patties hit the hot grease, a wonderful aroma filled the kitchen. She also enjoyed picking wild greens, dandelion, creasy and poke, especially, in spring while they were tender. She always cooked them with fat meat and served them doused with vinegar. On occasion, we would stop at Dorothea's house when returning from school and we always hoped there would be leftover biscuits in the covered, oval shaped, blue enamel roaster which sat on the cabinet. We had to ask permission if we wanted a biscuit. As a child, I heard many old wives' tales and superstitions repeated. The truth is, I didn't pay any attention to them, but Dorothea was quite superstitious in some of the things she said, such as, if you spill salt, pick it up and toss it across your shoulder. And you should leave the house through the same door you entered.

Sometimes Dorothea and Sam and Zan would walk the road and come up for a visit and have coffee with Momma and Daddy.

Sam and Daddy were such good friends and Sam proved his loyalty to their friendship when, on one occasion, our car caught fire on a cold morning when we were preparing to go to church. Daddy had gone out, started the car and came back in the house to wait for it to warm. Without warning, the car caught fire and the smoke and flames could be seen from down the hill where Sam lived. Knowing that my dad, exhausted from working the hoot owl shift, which is midnight to next morning, would sometimes fall asleep in his car, Sam ran up the hill and jerked the car door open with flames leaping at him and shouted, "Ivo, are you in there!" He literally risked his life for my dad. I am ever grateful for Sam and his brave compassion in that incident.

Had we chosen to take a prejudiced approach to people of different backgrounds, we would never have learned so much about their ethnicity.

We just lived diversity by the very fact we socialized with all the folks within the camp, many of whom were immigrants who arrived to seek out a livelihood. We were blessed to be surrounded by the richness of differences and the valuable investments of skilled individuals.

The sense of community was evident among the people, and we were instilled with the importance of respect for others, especially our elders. We were carefree to the extent we could roam about our mountains and camps without fear and our creativity was given free rein in those hillsides. If we decided to go for a walk on a summer day, we would leave the mountain and go down in the community and stroll on wooden sidewalks, stopping to chat with whomever happened to be out in the yard. Mrs. Himsley had a small store in the front room of her house which was a convenience to the residents. Bread and milk and other small essentials could be bought there. Sometimes we would buy penny candy which was weighed on a scale, and it was asked for by saying you wanted ten cents worth or whatever you had to spend. A bag of potato chips cost a nickel and a coke seven cents.

While spending time outdoors walking through the neighborhood, we knew to behave because there was always someone around ready to inform our parents if wrong actions warranted it. Neighbors became involved in a child's life as they played throughout the camp with other kids because many people were always in their yards or sitting on the porch enjoying a time of relaxation with their evening coffee and chatting with friends. They were the extra eyes for parents in the community.

Bottom Creek community ca. 1970
courtesy of ERCA

SCHOOL DAYS 1952-53
VIVIAN
Alma

Maitland 1929

Phylenia school photo, eleven years old, 1957-1958

1952 Ford Truck

Teddy and me at Easter

Although age has destroyed this house, it resembles. Sam and Dorothea's house many years ago.

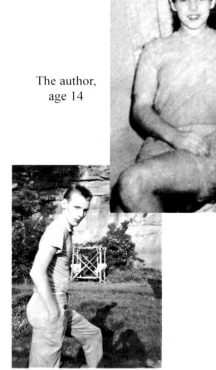

The author, age 14

Teddy and Eddie with our border collie, Kate

My boyfriend

Lives Interrupted

The coalfields were not without tragedy, either. Alma and I were returning home from school one spring day in 1955 and were stopped by the son of the camp's postmaster who informed us that our brother, Jackie who was only three years old, had been run over by a truck. Stricken with anxiety, tears, and bewilderment, we made our way across the railroad tracks and then onward to the hillside path. We began to verbalize our thoughts in a childish way and nervously hoped for no more than a broken bone or something of that nature. As we arrived home, stepping on to the front porch, our Momma ran toward us, grabbing us tightly and sobbing uncontrollably, "Jackie's dead! My baby is gone!"

Alma and I both cried while she hugged us, leaving us stunned and silent, not knowing how to respond with words.

In the moments and days that followed, there were many things I do not remember but a few have been indelibly etched on my mind and remain to this day.

The local newspaper reported on the accident. Daddy had taken a coal delivery to a man in Welch and parked on a narrow, one-way street. When a car approached, Daddy had to move the large truck. Jackie, thinking Daddy was going to leave, ran behind the truck and Daddy unknowingly ran over him! A dark, despairing cloud settled on our home life after that, for we all cherished our little brother. We, his siblings, were just getting to know him, this blond curly haired toddler. One memory vividly etched in my mind was a time when we all stood in the corner of the front yard where Jackie was standing on a large rock under the giant Locust tree. This was the spot where the whole camp came into view. We were teaching him to talk and laugh with us, excited with his presence and celebrating another member of our "gang." We watched as he toddled around the house and, on one occasion, he climbed up, barefooted, on the kitchen table and took the stick of butter from the dish and began to eat it causing laughter to erupt around the table, while Momma scolded. He was a beautiful little child. Sadness locked us in its grip for a long time…his passing left an empty chair at our breakfast table, and we knew no one could ever mimic his preciousness. Yet, we had to keep going forward; we were too young to engage in deep conversation about such a tragedy. We were handed an extremely, heart piercing life event and so it was that we had to continue to celebrate each other and with maturity we would need to settle into a state of acceptance of our painful loss.

    News of his death spread rapidly through the coal camp. Some may have learned the news by eavesdropping on the telephone because we had a two-party phone line. When someone's phone rang, long and short rings that came through on the other party's phone distinguished it, so it was quite easy to know when another person was on the phone. But just one spark of benevolence ignited the sympathies of all the residents in the camp. They began to call and file through our house to extend condolences, offering up many prayers of comfort and our pastor, Brother John, proved to be a loyal and constant presence during that time, bringing compassion to our house.

    Aunts and uncles arrived to bring solace to my parents. Even though I was only eight years old at the time, I vividly recall sitting on the front row of the chapel in the funeral home, smelling the flower arrangements which were mostly Carnations and to this day, I really do not like the fragrance of them. Strange how the mind plays tricks on you during grief. As I gazed numbly at my brother's still form, I thought he still was breathing, and I now realize that must have been a momentary denial stage of my grief.

    In the weeks and months that followed, it felt as if the dark haze would never lift from our family. Momaw spent much time with Momma in hearing her heart cries and expressions of deep sorrow. Momma said as she talked to Momaw about her feelings, Momaw said, "Lottie there is such a thing as a living sorrow." She was referring to the daily anguish of knowing her son, as he served in WW II, was on the battlefront, facing an unknown future. All of us experienced the full range of emotions as we endeavored to cope with our loss amid spewing anger, hatred, and resentment with streams of tears and then finally, acceptance comes. To "get over" a tragedy is not a fitting statement. Acceptance seems only to make it more bearable.

One day on my arrival home from school, I began to holler for Momma because I did not see her inside the house, so I made my way to the back porch where I found her sitting on the steps, sobbing inconsolably as she stared at pictures of my little brother. I remember the incident so well: "What's wrong, Momma?'

Shaking her head as she looked at the pictures in her hand, she said, "my baby's gone, and I'll never see him again."

I said, "But, Momma, you've got me."

She grabbed me and hugged me, saying, with shaky voice, "I know, honey, I know."

"Momma will you make me a sandwich please?"

"Yes, honey, let's get in the kitchen and do that now," she said taking me by the hand.

"And put a lid on it, please." Momma reminded me that was what I called the slice of bread that covered the sandwich.

Little children sometimes speak words of wisdom, not realizing the impact it can have on someone, Momma recounted this incident to me much later in life. And she shared from her heart the following: She said at times she felt as if she would literally lose her mind. She, at last decided to see a doctor who prescribed a medicine to calm her, but she also turned, in anguish of her heart, to the prayers of faith with her brothers and sisters. And, over time, they were her source of strength and healing from the cloud of depression that tried to consume her. Her deliverance came, she told me, when she knelt at an altar of prayer during a service conducted by a lady pastor who was a friend to our family. Momma said in that moment, when she put her hands on her and began to pray, it felt like a rock was lifted from her shoulders. A powerful testimony that brought joy to my soul. We kept moving forward and remembering with episodes of tear-filled grief until finally acceptance. Momma experienced deep grief when her first child died. A little girl named Etta Lee when she was only eight months old. She died of pneumonia Momma told me, but she had wondered at times if her death was due to an allergic reaction to the sulfa drug. It was the early forties and some antibiotics were still new treatments.

In 1960, five years following the loss of our baby brother, the phone rang in the middle of the night with the news that my fifteen-year-old brother Eddie, had been involved in a car wreck. He had been in Welch hanging out with friends, playing the jukebox at the Tic Toc Grill, and decided to hitchhike home. Not many teenagers had a car back in those days, so this was commonplace for the time. And there was a mutual trust among people during that time as well. A man from our community offered him a ride which he readily accepted, and the newspaper account stated that the driver was speeding. As a result, he sideswiped an oncoming car and struck the corner of a brick store building. The wife of the driver died, and my brother was thrown from the back seat toward the front and struck the dashboard.

My brother lay unconscious for over a week in the hospital, without much hope of full recovery. He was an innocent victim of someone else's carelessness. Our home life was once again disrupted, as Ma had to rearrange our house to accommodate a hospital bed for my brother who required extensive rehabilitative care at home. One side of his face had a deep cut down his cheek, and he had to have a rod placed in one leg where the bone was shattered. I do not recall how long the process of recovery required and I do not remember lots of dialogue, but exhaustion and stress were a weighty burden for Momma. But the one fact that stands out in looking back is the amount of energy and attention his condition demanded, I am sure we 'just knew' that was the way it had to be. And he did recover from the serious injuries.

Tragedies of this magnitude threaten to rob you of your stability and all you hold dear. They become dark, monstrous intruders into your home life. But during those times it was a great comfort to have friends and family who lent emotional, spiritual, and physical support as you walked through the pain toward healing. I was only thirteen at the time of this tragedy and I don't recall any fine details. Things just were not the same after that event. Over time, Eddie decided he did not want to complete his schooling and he left home as did my older brother and they became wanderers, independent thinkers, moving with their own ideas in mind, I suppose. I don't recall hearing parental discussions, but I know they would not have agreed with them. When they moved away, I lost contact with them. I continued in my education and the usual interests of a teenage girl, which would include a steady boyfriend. My youngest brother, Teddy remained and he and my older sister, Alma and I became a threesome. Interacting and growing up together, we continued our way of life with school, nearby friends, and home responsibilities.

I was closer to my youngest brother, Teddy. He was now the baby of the family and Momma doted over him as such. He became sick on one occasion with a croupy cough and Momma called the doctor to see if he would check him. Momma turned and said," the doctor can see him but he requires payment right then." That was a very anxious moment for Momma, so she proceeded with the usual home remedies and Teddy recovered quickly and all was fine.

He was content to be a loner, but he had friends that came to play marbles or croquet or to just go exploring.

Sometimes he would go visit his little classmates who lived on a hill opposite ours and it was visible from our front yard and we could yell in that direction and be heard easily. Teddy was intent on exploring the mountain as he found his place amid the vast curiosities of nature. Adding in those times of mischief that accompany childhood.

A friend and elementary school classmate of his, informed me that when he and my brother were in second grade, Teddy brought a snake to school (common garden) and came at him with the snake in hand, shaking it in his face, scaring him to death trying to start a fight with him. I did not know of this when we were kids.

Only in a recent year, after learning of my brother's passing, was I told this story because I had not been in contact with this childhood friend previously. But the account of the snake story warmed my heart as it brought to my memory an image of a bygone time in our childhood that meant so much to me. It was a surprising bittersweet memory of Teddy. Time passed, he grew up, joined the Navy, and served his term on the USS Coral Sea. I have his scarf to his dress white uniform and some postcards he sent as he served on ship. We went our separate ways with many miles of distance between us as we were nurturing and developing our own vocations and family lifestyle. He had no children but loved to travel and enjoy the outdoors as well. And he loved Lemon meringue pies, and he asked me to bake him one many years ago and I did. In his early childhood days, I found it strange that he ate "mustard" sandwiches made with two slices of bread, mustard slathered on and sprinkled with black pepper. I suppose that is why I loved him. He dared to be different. And he is missed greatly!

Home and Drugstore Remedies Remembered

We contracted the usual childhood diseases, chickenpox, mumps, and croup. Many old-time home remedies were relied upon, especially in the case of croup. Our Momma was no exception to those who resorted to folk remedies handed down through the years.

When we had croup, if we did not have those little, black croup pills, Momma made what she called a ginger and lemon "toddy" to drink. I do not remember all the ingredients, but lemon, ginger and sugar were the primary ones, and we had to sip it real hot. She would rub our chest with Vick's VapoRub, Musterole or camphorated oil and put a piece of warm flannel over it. Not only did the ointments work, but also Momma's loving concern could be felt in the soothing touch of her soft, tender hands.

To infections or boils, we applied an ointment that we called, simply, "black salve:" Turpentine was used to soak a nail wound on the foot. Old time, home remedies were common.

An ad for the Grand Ole Opry Country Music Show

So familiar an item in a woman's wardrobe

Jolly Time Popcorn

McCall's Pattern

Fleecy White Bleach

Octagon Soap

Maxwell House Coffee

Back porch wash day

Log Cabin Syrup Tin

Oh, the sound
and aroma of coffee perking
thru the glass top

Cabinet like ours

Blue Willow Dishes

Friday night boxing match on television

Vintage television

Mason Jars

Bobby Socks

Phone with no rotary dial

Fly Spray that was pumped into the air

Leather Britches

Rusty Coal Bucket

Civil Defense Sign

Lard Bucket

Majestic Coal-Fired Wood Stove

Lawn Mower

Signs of the Times and Activities on the Home Front

Materially speaking, we did not have excesses or the fanciest, but our needs were being met very well and we had our Momma's love which she was quick to express to us kids. She took pride in her cooking and in her efforts to provide pretty clothes which she ordered occasionally from Sears, Roebuck.

She was quick to embrace us when we "got the croup," or any other malady for that matter, and she spoke comforting words and reassured us that she would make us better. My heartwarming recollections of her presence, I have cherished in my heart and locked them away as precious jewels.

Every season of mountain living brings with it, new opportunities to explore, to create! Surrounded by the vastness of nature and the way each season of the year exhibits beauty as if on a runway of newly designed fashions, there was much to discover no matter which direction you looked. I remember gathering Black Walnuts and how valuable they were so we went in search of as many as we could gather and on occasion, when we would have surplus, we would sell them. People gathered them in large burlap sacks for home use. They were difficult to crack open and not until we removed the soft, outer, dark green peel that stained our fingers an orange, brown color. At our house, Momma used those Walnuts in fudge and in applesauce cakes she made around the Christmas holiday.

Just as the changing of seasons in nature exhibits a unique beauty for the occasion, my Momma's love did likewise as her compassion was evident when we were sick. And in good times, joyous laughter pealed through the house as she baked and cooked and sang along with radio programs, while teaching us from her life experiences and welcoming our curiosities of life.

I cannot think about my childhood without remembering those attributes of my Momma.

Her role in our family influenced my development because she never discouraged me from trying to learn from her. She exemplified a woman with endurance to weather the storms of life, as we discovered in the tragedies that occurred.

And on the lighter side...

The time came that I needed to learn to make bubbles from bubble gum. I could not figure out how the grown-ups were doing that. I took my momma captive in her room and lying cross ways on the bed, I insisted that she stay put until I had this down to a science. Every time I took her jaws in my pudgy hands and said, "do it again", she laughed at me because of my determination. And so, she stayed with the task until I gave her "permission" to leave my presence. Now that I'm an adult who enjoys reading the Scriptures, this event with my Momma reminds me of Jacob who wrestled with an Angel at Bethel and said, "I will not let you go until you bless me!" Of course, my momma being the angel in this scene...Mission accomplished.

Momma allowed me to get "under foot" too, as she lovingly prepared our meals. As a young child, I so loved watching her mix a batch of homemade rolls on that old kitchen cabinet with the built-in flour bin and sifter and the pull-out enamel top on which she kneaded the bread. She then placed that large lump of dough in a Jewel Tea, Autumn Leaf design crock bowl, which she covered with a cloth and placed on a chair behind the cook stove where the warmth would cause the dough to rise. It is a wonder that people from miles around did not get a whiff of those wonderful rolls baking in the oven and ascend to the mountain where we lived!

Our Majestic cookstove had to be fired up until it reached the required temperature for whatever food was being baked. Homemade chocolate cakes and stuffed green peppers were baked in that coal fired oven as well; it is no wonder the preacher loved to come to Sunday dinner! And Momma enjoyed trying new recipes and she discovered one that fit perfectly with our Thanksgiving holiday meal. It was the recipe for sweet potato croquettes. I watched as she mashed the cooked sweet potatoes and added vanilla and a little brown sugar, cinnamon, and an egg. She then shaped into a ball, pressing an indention in the center where she placed a large marshmallow and used more potato to cover it. She coated the sweet potato ball in crushed corn flakes and then baked them.

    I love to re-visit Momma's kitchen from time to time. My memory is still infused with the Appalachian influence, and I love cooking and baking, as did my momma. I thought about my momma and the process involved in her making breakfast. She would have sifted flour from the pull-down bin in her cabinet, then reached underneath the porcelain top, behind the larger door and brought out a two-pound bucket of lard and added a measure of that to the flour. She would then mix in the fresh buttermilk, which she sometimes bought from a family who lived on the mountain and kept cows and grew produce for sale. Once the dough was shaped into a lump, it was then rolled out with a rolling pin to a good thickness for tall, flaky biscuits. She cut them using a Carnation milk can which had the top removed to create a biscuit cutter. The end result was some of the best biscuits you ever sank your teeth into. Then she would bring out the large, family size, iron skillet, add cooking grease she saved from the streaked bacon she fried, then flour, and make a roux (we called it a thickener) then pour the milk, salt and pepper and stand over the stove and stir, stir, stir, slowly so as not to get splattered by the bubbling, hot gravy.

    In the right time of year, she would cook apples, (apples gathered as we roamed our mountain), with brown sugar and cinnamon, which we loved to eat on our buttered-with-real butter, biscuits or, sometimes, Momma's blackberry jelly.

Momma would have set the table with Blue Willow dishes and coffee cups, but the silverware was a random collection of forks and knives and spoons. But who noticed? Who really cared when you were eating such wonderful food?

Our house was furnished quite simply with only the basics. No carpet in our house but linoleum flooring. We had no automatic washer or dryer. Consequently, wash day was a laborious and a dreaded task that might be due in part to the size of the family. Monday's wash day was accompanied by putting a pot of brown beans on the stove to cook throughout the day and have them ready for supper by the time the wash was finished. I can hear Momma lift the lid of the bean pot and pour hot water from the tea kettle that was used for adding water to the beans.

Wash day involved filling the washer with water and adding detergent and Fleecy White bleach in the case of white items. Then we filled the rinse tub and let the clothes that passed through the wringer drop in for a rinsing. Once rinsed, we passed the clothing back through the wringer and then one load of wash was ready for the clothesline. The process continued throughout the day. The wringer washer and the rinse tub had to be refilled when the wash water became dirty or the rinse water too soapy, in preparation for the next load of clothes. A bottle of bluing which, when added to the rinse water, made colored clothes brighter and whites whiter. The clean laundry was hung out on a clothesline and then each piece was removed after it dried, carried in and made ready for ironing. Daddy installed pulleys and stretched our clothesline from the back porch to a pole set up in the backyard. It was a convenience to stand on the porch and send the clothes out on a line to dry. Occasionally, Momma used a thick, block of brown Octagon laundry soap for heavy duty cleaning. When it was rubbed over very soiled places on clothing it emitted a strong almost medicinal smell, unlike the aromatic fragrances of laundry detergents today. Starch was purchased in a box and mixed with hot water and there was a small, blue, block of additive for the starch called Satina, which made ironing so much smoother. Clean laundry such as blouses and shirts was drenched in the starch, wrung, and hung out to dry. Crocheted doilies were commonly used on end tables in homes and Momma would make a heavy starch solution for dipping the doily and then she used a glass or teacup as a form to wrap each ruffle of the doily so it could stand alone, thus creating an artistic masterpiece to be displayed in the living room. At the end of wash day, it was time to stir up a skillet of corn bread, slide it into that Majestic coal fired cookstove and supper was ready. That is, once the cornbread was done. We loved Momma's cornbread that we crumbled in the buttermilk and ate with supper sometimes.

The old and often used No.3 washtub provided numerous services around the coalfield house. It was not uncommon to place it behind the cook stove and fill it with water for bathing. We did have indoor plumbing, but not a bathroom, just the infamous outhouse. Granted, there was no privacy since many houses of that time, especially in the coalfields, did not have doors separating the rooms, but curtains, which were usually made of heavy cotton or possibly plastic. Until Daddy built a shower room, we learned to improvise by hanging a towel from the stove to the door of the kitchen. It was just understood when bath time was happening; you stayed clear of the room. Many people kept rain barrels at the corner of their house to catch water for various reasons. We always loved to wash and rinse our hair in rainwater because it made our hair silky soft.

In winter weather, the coal-fired, Majestic cook stove in the kitchen and the big, Warm Morning heater which sat on a large, tin fireproof mat in the living room, served extra duty. It was not unusual to go in a house in the winter and find clothesline strung in the kitchen for drying clothes. Should the weather turn extremely cold with lots of snow on the ground, water pipes would likely freeze. We drew upon our ability to be resourceful; using what was at hand, by melting snow in a washtub on top of the stove to have water for household uses. After a heavy snowfall in winter, we looked forward to making snow ice cream, which was done by mixing clean snow with sugar, vanilla, and evaporated milk.

Our house, situated on a hill, with a cliff behind it and the camp's water supply tank beside it, was of simple wooden construction with no insulation in the walls. Therefore, the frigid temperatures and blustery wind gusts caused a layer of ice to form on the windows in my and my sister Alma's bedroom and she and I spoke in frosted breath as we said, "good night." When the winds howled around our house and through the screen on the window, we heard loud screeching sounds that scared us when they were unexpected.

We were kept warm in the blankets we heated by wrapping them around the Warm Morning heater in the living room. We clutched our blanket tightly and hurried to our bedroom so as not to lose the heat. Then Momma would throw a green, heavy wool, Army blanket across our bed. That blanket sealed in the warmth, and we would drift into a cozy slumber, but not until we caught up on our sister talks about a friend's brother who was nice looking or the current romance problems of another friend in school. Or who would get a Valentine from us.

The fire in the living room stove was banked at night; this was done by pouring slack on it and adjusting the damper so it would burn slowly, allowing enough fire for a strong start the next day. But the cook stove had to be re-started each morning. Getting up to an extremely cold house was not an especially welcomed event!

Wood for burning had to be chopped to fit the stoves and coal had to be shoveled in buckets and carried inside the night before to prepare for the next day's cooking and heating.

Most of the time it was required that the boys in the family did this chore, but I always welcomed the challenge of wielding an axe to a chopping block and loading a bucket full of black nuggets to prove to myself I could do it. And I did...but! On one occasion I took on the challenge of chopping wood, while I was barefoot and nearly cut my toe off. I bled like a stuck hog! I found an old rag lying by the coal box and wrapped my toe in it to stop the bleeding. I would not even tell my mom and dad about it because I did not want to go to the doctor! I waited until late evening when I was sure the doctor's office was closed before I revealed my plight to them.

If we chose to be lazy, we endured unpleasant consequences! If the wood and coal were not carried in at night before bedtime and a big snow or rain fell, the dampened wood was extremely hard to ignite. It was a real challenge to get a fire going. And we had to have a fire if we were going to cook breakfast. We have put everything on wood trying to kindle a fire: from meat fat to granulated sugar! And all had to be accomplished while shivering from head to toe! Creating a fire in the stove was not the end of the process. As the coal burned, ashes fell through the grate, which held the wood and coal in place and the grate had to be shaken sometimes. The pan that contained the ashes then had to be removed and emptied to allow for good combustion. The ashes were collected and poured by the coal house (box to some) and reserved for use by pouring over slick spots during a snow. They gave excellent traction when needed for the car tires on snowy days.

Our water was heated by the coal-stove method. A large, cylindrical water tank with pipes was attached to the kitchen stove so that when a fire was built, the water heated. On one end of the cook stove was a reservoir for water that also heated as the fire burned and that was handy for dishes and smaller chores around the house.

Since many families were larger in number, it was more economical to make meals from scratch. Our kitchen table was handmade by Daddy and sat next to the window that faced the back yard and the cliff. When company came to eat with us, Momma spread an oil cloth table covering over the top. She created a pretty setting for us to enjoy. Breakfast consisted of hot homemade biscuits, with gravy and jelly or apple butter. It had a stick-to-your ribs quality. Alma loved onions with her gravy and biscuits, preferring them over the jelly and apple butter.

We considered it a real treat to have boxed cereal for breakfast. Momma made genuine hot cocoa for our breakfast too. I vividly recall seeing Momma, so attentive to the needs of her kids, bring the Hershey's cocoa from the cabinet measuring it out along with sugar into a large cup, She then lifted the teakettle with steaming water from the cast iron surface of the coal stove and poured it into the cup leaving enough room to add the Carnation milk. The spoon tapping the side of the cup as she stirs tells me the rich chocolate drink is ready, ahh. And I loved to dip my toast in the hot cocoa; how tasty that was! Homemade pancakes with syrup poured from a tin, Log Cabin shaped container, crisp bacon, and the wonderful, aroma of coffee perking on the coal stove. Not only the bubbling sound of water being sent through the stem of the coffee filter, but the added aroma filled our kitchen, leaving an indelibly etched and soothing memory on our souls. Was it our young taste buds or was it the quality of the product? But it seems to me that those foods we enjoyed during childhood tasted better then, even the peanut butter and jelly sandwiches!

The white, wooden cabinet which contained a pull-down flour bin with a sifter attached, was a very practical item in the kitchen. The enameled surface when extended forward provided a useful place for kneading and rolling breads and pie dough.

When Momma made cakes and icing, we raced to see who would get to sop the bowl! The manual, rotary mixer was good for a lickin' as well. Sopping the bowl was just a tasty prelude to the finished product Momma would bring from the coal-fired oven.

Early coalfield life was a preview of the concept of recycling because we learned to save jelly, salad dressing and pickle jars for drinking glasses. I can remember thinking I would feel "fancy" if I could just sit at a table with matched dishes and glasses. I do recall the set of Blue Willow dishes we owned for a time, but they lacked the durability of dinnerware today. And, too, I suppose we kids were a typically rambunctious type where anything delicate in nature, such as glassware would meet with destruction! Anyway, my Momma's cooking was so tasty; the need for matched place settings paled in comparison.

At Christmas time we had the privilege of going to the mountains and cutting our own tree. And like most kids, we had high hopes for snowfalls that we could enjoy.

We always took advantage of the snowy season, making our road into a ski slope so we could slide down the hill in our galoshes or go barreling down in a shovel. The snow was excellent for winter activities, not forgetting the sculpting of a snowman and throwing snowballs! Momma bought the electric lights one year that were strung to sit on the branches of the tree and there was a candle in the center that bubbled when the lights warmed. And we designed our own wreaths and evergreen decorations with what was available; tree branches, pinecones and roughly designed candy canes and stars cut out of cardboard and colored with crayons or covered with aluminum foil. We colored notebook paper giving each line a different color and then we cut each strip, gluing the ends together creating links and fashioning a chain for our tree. We had to exercise some creativity to bring a festive air to the holidays. And we decorated our tree and house with festive flair of celebration.

And, whether there was snow or not during Christmas, Momma bought a can of spray snow and stencils, and we created our own designs on the windows to make it appear that snowy weather was with us. The most common gifts I remember were dolls for girls, and cowboy themed toys like cap guns with holsters for boys. The caps came in rolls and could be bought year-round. Sometimes for a larger noise, kids would place a roll of caps on the walkway and use a large rock for louder impact and cause the whole roll to fire at once. And fringed gloves with cowboy names on them were popular for some time. Girls loved costume jewelry and shiny, plastic stone, red or green rings, tea sets with dishes. Alma received a camera one Christmas and the boys received sometimes sports items like a basketball or football, new boots, and socks. We also loved puzzles and the Monopoly game was popular.

We were not accustomed to luxurious gifts at Christmas time, but a special gift. There was one time when Alma and I were convinced that we were getting absolutely nothing. I recall that Daddy and Momma spoke of the slack work conditions, explaining the reason that money was in short supply and told us, cautiously, not to expect anything. But Daddy surprised us on Christmas morning with a small doll for each of us. Oh, how we cherished that gift! And we held them near to our heart and took good care of and kept them for many years of play. And the smiles on Momma and Daddy's faces said that they knew we would be happy with our gift.

We also looked forward to the holiday purchase of mixed nuts in the shell. We had a bowl designed to hold the nutcracker and the picks and we would enjoy the variety of English Walnuts, Filberts, and Pecans. `Through the holiday, we also enjoyed Chocolate drops and Chocolate covered cherries. It was the one time of the year that Momma and Daddy splurged on the candy. Christmas was a time of excitement for us kids. From the search for a tree to the creative art in decorations, we immersed ourselves in every way we could to keep the holiday joy bubbling in our house.

Summertime came and found us working the land to raise fresh vegetables. Daddy plowed a garden spot around the side of the hill from where our house stood. Out of the mountain, a fresh, water spring flowed nearby. The water was always ice cold and delicious. Once school was out for the summer, Momma would get up early, make breakfast and then call out to all of us, "Come on kids! Eat breakfast so we can get out and pull those weeds and hoe before the sun gets too hot." And I chattered to her as we made those midsummer jaunts from our house around the mountain side to tend the garden.

When harvest time came, we helped Momma pull the ears of corn, collect the tomatoes that had ripened and gather green beans. What joy to think about those times in the mountain. What blessings we gave thanks for! Living off the land that produced a bounty of veggies, fruits, and nuts. And that mountain for me was a vast classroom, not only of much learning in nature, but it created an appreciation for the importance of responsibility. Daddy dug out a cellar, building it with cinder block and wooden shelves that held the many beautiful jars of preserved foods that Momma put up for winter.

When we lived in Bottom Creek, I remember that a produce truck would come through the community, park on the side of the road and give residents an opportunity to buy fresh vegetables. Momma sent me to inquire of the salesman about what he had to offer. And I came back and told her that he said he has, Irish potatoes, sweet potatoes and mashed potatoes, then laughter erupted as I tried to imitate the salesman's rapid speech.

We did not keep farm animals except I recall that we did own one hog and remember that in the fall of one year, someone came and helped Daddy in the butchering of it and then they divided the pork for preserving for the families. Momma made fried pork skins that were a treat, just as potato chips were. And she rendered the lard and stored it for use in her cooking. Mountain living required hard work in every season, but the vastness of our mountains also presented us with endless opportunities for creative thinking, whether in work or play. These were our mountains.

Miner's payday was every two weeks. It was then that Momma went to Welch to the Kroger store to buy the staples for cooking. And she would browse the department stores as well. Before she left to go to town though, she would ask each of us what we would like her to buy as a special treat. I chose Kraft caramels because there were so many in a bag and individually wrapped. When she brought them home, I made a secret place in my chest of drawers and hid them there so they would last for days. The Kroger store would mark down their baked goods every Saturday, and we could get two loaves of bread for fifty-cents, packages of cinnamon rolls would be half price. Stores were not open on Sunday back then, so grocers wanted fresh baked goods on Monday. On the road to Welch and not far from our house, there was a spring on the side of the road that had an easy access. Many people took advantage of the water spring flowing from the mountain. And many times, Daddy would stop and fill a couple of gallon jugs and bring us some of that water. A pipe was installed at some point in time to make it easier to fill jugs. That spot was used by many folks over the years and it is talked about even today.

Back Porch Friends, Pin Curls, and Coalfield Life

Living in the coalfields brought the most unique style of living for us. As kids, we roamed freely in the mountains and while Daddy went to work in the mines, the women of the coal fields formed a strong bond among themselves, creating a camaraderie unlike any other.

The camps were designed in such a way, that children of families became classmates from elementary school to graduation from high school and the women, those strong women, formed their own coffee klatch; they were decades ahead of the coffee shop social gathering.

There were times I remember so well. Those who shared in the same denominations attended church together and there were women's societies formed within the church that ministered in many ways to missionaries at home and abroad. And some were involved in charity organizations outside the church.

Once the kids were off to school, the women gathered to have coffee, exchange recipes or cut and style each other's hair. Pin curls were the fashion back then. I never did understand how Momma managed to reach behind her head, twist a curl and slide a bobby pin through her hair. On occasion, the women were known to share "just a little bit" of neighborly gossip.

I give you a typical scene as it might have been for a housewife who is being visited by her neighbor so that you can listen in to a sample of what may have been heard as one such day occurred.

Viv hears the footsteps approaching on the back porch and as her neighbor walks in---

"Hey, Sadie, the coffee's ready. And be sure the screen door closes, don't want flies getting in here."

Like everyone we meet, the greeting opens with discussion about the weather...

"Did you hear the thunder last night?" Sadie asked.

"Yeah, Viv said. Came a good rain, didn't it?"

Sadie walks over to the stove to pour her coffee; "So whatcha been up to, Viv ?" she asks as the tinkling sound of the spoon against her cup blends the milk in her coffee. Then she sits at the kitchen table.

"Well, not much." Viv says. Have some more canning to do and gathering in the rest of the garden. Not much left but I can make some end of garden pickles with what's there."

"My momma used to make those pickles," Sadie noted. These were times when nothing was wasted and everything that could possibly be preserved, well, it was preserved. And used through the winter.

"I know what you mean, Sadie. We must watch the money, because we never know when there might be a lay-off or a strike, nor how long it could last."

Glancing up at the clock on the wall, "Guess I'd better get goin', Sadie said as she turned up her cup of "good to the last drop" coffee. Got to get down to the company store and pick up a couple of things before the young 'uns get home from school. Thanks for the coffee."

"Oh, well, if you must go. Say howdy to everybody for me." Let me know when you want your hair done so I can put aside the time for it." "I will," Sadie replies

"And I'm glad to hear your family's doing well. Y'all come on over the first chance you get and we'll sit in the swing and tell some of those tales I've been itching to talk about...like the time Aunt Flossie went out to milk the cows and stepped in a fresh cow pie. Whew! Good thing she kept a spare pair of old garden shoes in the tobacco barn. They saved the day."

"Take care, now, Viv. I may run in to you at the company store and we'll just catch up on politics and raisin' kids and Lord knows, what else, there by the produce shelves."

"Come back anytime" Viv yells, as the screen door slams shut.

And the morning has opened with conversation, inspiration, and coffee. A good place to begin the day of work that lies ahead.

No. 75.—LETTERS OF GUARDIANSHIP—Printed and for sale by Edwards & Broughton, Printers and Binders, Raleigh, N. C.

SURRY ~~Surry~~ COUNTY--In the Superior Court.

The State of North Carolina,

To all whom these Presents shall come==GREETING:

It being Certified to the Undersigned, Clerk of the Superior Court for Surry County, that Philena (Phylenia) Snow (formerly Golding) is a minor orphan, is without Guardian, and Bird Snow having applied for the guardianship of said minor child, and having been duly qualified as such:

Now, these are therefore to Authorize and Empower the said Guardian to enter in and upon all and singular, the goods and chattels, rights and credits of said minor orphan wheresoever to be found, and the same to take into possession, secure and improve, and further to manage said estate and every part thereof, for the benefit and advantage of the said minor orphan, and according to law.

WITNESS, my hand and the seal of said Court, this the 10th day of Dec. 1900

C. A. Haynes
Clerk Superior Court.

That's Entertainment!

Before everyone in the camp had television sets, friends would gather at a designated house on Saturday nights for favorite programs. One of the television programs I remember looking forward to enjoying with my friends was Highway Patrol with Broderick Crawford.

It was not unusual to hear a child asking, "Momma can I go down to Frankie's house and watch television?" There was always an affirmative reply because our parents knew that we would only be gone long enough to enjoy a television program, a single program and back to the house.

Then by the time wrestling became a big deal we had a television in our house. I was in third grade when Daddy bought our first television. I remember that he had to buy wires, antenna, and ribbon for connecting. And he walked up the mountain side and stood on the edge of the cliff for someone to throw the wire up to him. He then took it to very top of the mountain and connected it to the antenna that had been mounted in a tree. And soon we became the gathering spot for neighbors and friends. On the nights of the wrestling matches there was such whooping and hollering like you have never heard before. The most popular wrestler's name I remember from that time was a blonde-haired man named, "Gorgeous George". I don't remember other stage names at that time. It was everyone's emotional reactions to what was happening on television that impressed me the most.

Daddy enjoyed the Friday night boxing match on television. I still have vivid recollections of hearing the announcer say it was time for the "Cavalcade of Sports" sponsored by Gillette and introduced by a jingle which blared "Look sharp, feel sharp and be sharp, too." We all had our favorites in the television programs that were offered on the couple of channels we received.

And we kids had our brand of play and entertainment. When the hula hoop became all the rage, we couldn't wait to get one. Cousin Thelma who lived in North Carolina, came to visit on one occasion and surprised us with hula hoops. We were fascinated when she told us that she worked in the factory that made them. She gained instant celebrity status with us. We entertained ourselves for hours twirling that hoop around our waist and making it balance in motion so it would not drop, and we used it like a jump rope as it was easy to swing over our arms. Great fun for us and our friends! We kids across the tracks and on the mountain side, gained popularity among our peers when they learned that our cousin made hula hoops!

Once the school year closed, we gladly exchanged the smell of chalk dust on felt erasers, Crayons and pencil shavings, for the scent of the rich earth in the mountains and the woodsy smell of the mature trees that awaited our adventures.

We spent summer outdoors most of the time and we also enjoyed croquet and marbles as well, which were a tournament event among the coal camp kids. Rough and dirty knuckles were the evidence of marble shooting matches. Inevitably, there arose bickering about the use of "steelies" or oversized regulation marbles because they could bust up larger numbers of the smaller ones in the ring. Owning your own bag or pocketful of marbles gave bragging rights. Some kids made a hobby of trading them for certain designs, cat eye for example were highly sought after but most were solid colors with minimal markings. So, we had our brand of "Wall Street" traders (on a small scale) in the heart of the coal fields.

Amazing! The things we remember from childhood. As I reflect on those times, I place myself there, in my youth, watching the events all over and it includes the chatter, the squeals, and yes, the threats of those kids who are determined to win "this round" of marbles. There was always time for hide and seek or dodge ball. We girls loved to jump rope and we didn't need a store bought one. We would use worn out electrical cords for jumping rope sometimes. And the Jacks game provided lots of entertainment and could be played alone. It was a good way to exercise coordination because it required, once the ball was bounced, that the player pick up the jacks before the ball landed.

These were my mountains where I enjoyed the ever-changing scene of events, my West Virginia Mountains. On one occasion Teddy and I, along with a couple of our friends who lived on the opposite hillside from us, were outdoors, hanging out with our Collie, Major who was always close by. We were talking and minding our own business when suddenly there appeared a huge Black Snake and the boys with loud excited voices began to yell, "Git 'em! Major! So Major had to make several attempts to get the snake in his mouth, flinging it back and forth very strongly and rapidly until he had defeated it. We were witnessing our dog at work to protect us kids. He followed us on our berry picking adventures as well.

Interestingly, we learned that the news agency in Welch would bring new comic books with cover removed and empty them at the slate dump a short distance from our house. When we spotted them coming across the tracks down in the camp, we would make our way to the dump and salvage our favorites from the variety they emptied there. We greatly enjoyed the 'funny' books, as we called them. It was another form of recreation for us. I especially liked Nancy and Sluggo and Dagwood and Blondie and Archie and Veronica comics. And it was also a method of honing our reading skills.

Summertime also added a pleasant touch to all the hard chores, like washing, etc. Warm weather seemed to make housekeeping and cleaning a little more pleasant also. Since our house was quite simple, our floor covering was linoleum. We did not use a vacuum cleaner, but a broom and mop for cleaning. Our porches were wooden, and I enjoyed scrubbing them. My sister, Alma and I would place the Philco radio in the window and plug it in to the living room outlet and then we enjoyed listening to the music from "Your Hit Parade," aired by the local station, as we worked. So this was an opportunity to make a dual purpose of a chore. My sister and I could take off our shoes, roll up the legs of our jeans and do a few dance moves as we enjoyed the water we sprayed on the porch which was sprinkled with soap powder. As the broom was vigorously swished through the water, the mix of wet straw and soapy water created such a clean smell and made the dance moves a little smoother, but we had to be cautious about the splinters that were naturally a part of the wood. We never stopped to consider what sort of presentation we were performing for the people that lived down in the camp or cars traveling across Route 52, for there was no tree growth that shielded us and our house from plain view, and the music echoed from the mountainside as we danced.

There was a small creek that coursed its way through the community and during hotter temperatures it was refreshing to go barefoot and walk through the water as we searched for minnows and crawdads. We took along an empty can so we could catch them for a closer look to study their behavior. Our curious natures and a vast mountain filled with endless entertainment were a perfect match during our formative years in the mountains.

As the heat of summertime temperatures stretched out before us, we gladly welcomed Momma's homemade lemonade which she produced with freshly-squeezed lemons. After removing the seeds, she sliced the rinds and dropped them in the pitcher. Besides the juicy bits of pulp mixed with each mouthful, it was just as refreshing to take the sweetened rind from your glass and peel away every remaining morsel of fruit. Momma bought a hand cranked ice crusher to hang on the kitchen wall and it was perfect for those hot summer days and our lemonade.

Hot weather also brought back the usual insects that invaded houses. Not every house was protected by screen doors, so war was declared anew against summer pests! It seems so primitive now and hazardous when I think that folks used sticky fly paper suspended from the ceiling and cans with a handle that had to be pumped to release the fly spray into the air.

Another multi-purpose item found around coalfield homes was the burlap sack. Their durability made them useful for doormats placed on the porch to wipe dirty feet. They were also used for gathering Chinquapins and the Black Walnuts in the fall which women preserved for adding to their holiday goodies such as applesauce cakes and fudge. I also remember that beggars showed up in coal camps toting a burlap sack for collecting canned foods from any resident who would contribute.

We always looked forward to blackberry picking in the summer accompanied by one or the other of our pets. Our bravest family pet was a beautiful, black and brown Collie named Major. Kate was a red and white Border Collie of meeker, obedient temperament, which she displayed as she nursed some orphaned kittens that had arrived at our house. She was more apt to stay at home while Major followed us around the hillside and through the brier patches.

We felt a reassured sense of protection with him along because we had watched him, in amazement one day, display his power when he killed a snake just outside our yard! We would put on high-top boots, take our two- and five-pound lard buckets and pick berries all over the hillside. There were occasions over the years that we would pick washtubs full of blackberries. We were warned over and over to beware of snakes (the reason for boots in summer). Fortunately, we never encountered any during those long hot days out in the briers, but if we did, we knew Major would come to the rescue.

It was during those days of berry picking that our brothers taught us to whittle out a slingshot from a small, forked tree branch. A piece of old rubber inner tube from a tire was cut to complete the slingshot. And we learned we could use hollow-stemmed plants to carve out a whistle. We had a taste of entrepreneurship when we occasionally sold some of our berries for the magnificent sum of fifty cents a gallon!

Picking berries was only the beginning of the work. For, once we got them home, we had to help Momma clean, or "look" them as we called it, and pull the stems. Once that was done, we had to assemble the canning jars, wash them, sterilize them and have them ready for the jam and jelly that was about to be produced.

We did not mind the berry picking; it was quite delightful! But once it was time to begin preparations for canning, an argument might ensue over the washing of jars. That was too much like washing the dishes after a meal. I have never understood why dishwashing seemed to be such a contemptible chore. But inevitably, it seemed the kitchen sink was the place of sibling conflict. My sister, Alma and I found it hard to come to an agreement over who would wash and who would dry dishes! To keep the decision fair and square, as we called it, sometimes it was necessary to draw straws, the method used many times in pronouncing a judgment. We would, at last, work in unity, creating laughter over some tidbit of nonsense. Sometimes we played the radio as we worked and sang along to familiar tunes, which made the work more pleasant.

We knew not to spend too much time dawdling foolishly about a necessary job! After all, fresh fruit had to be processed quickly to avoid waste.

Finally, the berries were cooked to extract the juice, then strained by pouring through cheesecloth. The juice was put back on the stove with sugar added and when it came to a boil, pectin was added so it would gel. The berries canned for pies and cobblers tasted delightful when they were mixed with milk and poured over a homemade biscuit.

Whenever Momma had to process large amounts of canned foods, a circular, outdoor fireplace was made with rocks to support a washtub. In the tub, were arranged the jars Mom had cold-packed with green beans or peaches or tomatoes, whatever happened to be ready for canning. Then water was added to the proper depth and a fire was kept under the tub for the required time to safely preserve the food.

To take a break from these work times, our idea of playing was to pack a picnic which consisted of maybe a biscuit sandwich with tomatoes or jelly and a Mason jar filled with Kool-Aid and head off to the mountains to play and pretend. I can still smell the mossy green carpeting around the base of tree trunks as I enjoyed inspecting the Toadstools that made their homes there. As we sat beneath the Rhododendron canopy, we pretended to be inside a tent. We learned to identify birch trees and always sought them out so we could break a young, tender twig and gnaw on the sweet bark. The cool mountain air provided blessed relief during the summer heat! Wild grapevines hung from the trees, creating an excellent swing and we couldn't walk by them without testing their stability so we could toss the vine out away from the tree and then as it swung back, we would catch it in a tight grip and ride for a distance and then push off at the nearest tree trunk for momentum to keep swinging. What fun in the mountains! We also learned about wildflowers by taking to the mountains for recreation. I can only recall the beautiful colors, deep, scarlet reds, purples, and orange blooms surrounded us. At the time, of course, I could not have named them, but I now know they were Trilliums, Mountain Azaleas, Violets, Jewelweed, Spiderwort and Lady Slippers.

The mountains were a splendid place of education, wonderment, and fantasy, where spirit, soul and body were revived. And we always made our way out before dark.

I am sure that knowing our Momma was at home and would be there if we needed her, provided the security we needed as we ventured into the mountains. Although, when we were older, on rare occasions, Momma ironed and did housecleaning for several families in nearby communities. I can remember going to a house on one occasion where Momma worked and when I opened the fridge to get water, I spotted lots of goodies used in baking and thought from my childlike perspective that these folks must be rich. Truth was Momma always cooked great meals, including good desserts like chocolate cake and cream pies that would rival anyone's skills.

Eventually Momma became a nursing assistant in a local hospital and found the work quite rewarding, as she was able to exercise her gifts of mercy and compassion in this vocation. We were fortunate that she did not have to work full time outside the home throughout our childhood.

On Saturday morning as teen-agers, we would look forward to going to the record hop, sponsored by the local radio station, WELC and emceed by one of their Deejays, Russ Cooke. The Saturday morning record hop was held on the stage of the Pocahontas movie theater in Welch. It was a wonderful time of socializing and making new friends and dancing the morning away. And, if permission was `given, we could stay in town to see a movie following the record hop which went off the air at one o'clock in the afternoon. After the movies, we could stroll along the streets and window shop or stop in at a locally owned restaurant or café where homemade sandwiches, hot dogs, hamburgers, or chili were always five-star quality.

On rare occasions we would go to a movie at the Starland Drive-in, located in Big Four. There was a café called the Chatter Box not far from the theater and it was a popular eating place for the local folks.

Summertime was filled with wholesome activity that included congregating with classmates at nearby drive-ins for our favorite shakes and playing the jukebox. We would make our way to the G.C. Murphy store in Welch to hang out and browse the different departments. A visit there was like stepping into a wonderland, the colors, the lights, the aromas filled the air. Sweet candy vapors met you at the door. I enjoyed the beautiful jewelry that imitated shiny diamonds and the green emeralds and red ruby colors that sparkled under the lights. There were boxed sets of perfumes(think Evening in Paris), and for men there were boxed cologne and shave cream sets (think Old Spice). And, then there was the record department for listening to the latest hits. Toys filled a large corner and we paused to fill our imaginations. We attended street dances at the Howdy House drive-in as well. Another great social event for us teen-agers. Sometimes we would drive to the by-pass and stop at the lookout point and admire the romantic effect of the night lights of Welch. Saturday and Sunday were the only days my boyfriend came to visit. On Saturday he came in late afternoon and sometimes had a meal with us. At Momma's insistence. She believed if you came to our house, you should sit down to a meal with the family. He was allowed to stay until eleven o'clock but Sunday night he had to leave at ten o'clock during the school year. Our courtship was centered around my family activities because I was so young. My boyfriend would drive his '52 Ford pickup truck to my house. When I was around fourteen, he decided to begin teaching me how to drive. But first he wanted to teach me how to park the truck, using the space we had on the hill. Teddy and his friends, Larry, and Alan were playing together on this Saturday. And when they thought I was going to go for a drive in the truck, they jumped in the back. But about the time I started in reverse, I let the clutch out too quickly, the truck made a strong jerk forward and it scared the boys so badly that they jumped out of the truck bed. They thought I was going over the side of the mountain. What an outburst of laughter they caused. On another occasion my hubby did let me drive his truck through the camp so he could teach me how to change gears. Just another page in our courtship and knowing how to drive a truck with a straight stick.

Philco Radio

Jack Rocks

Picking Blackberries

Pocahontas theater where hubby and I first met in person

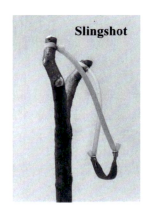

Playing Marbles

School Days

I began my education at Vivian Grade School while we lived in Bottom Creek. Then during my first grade, we moved to Maitland where I continued my first-grade experience.

Our early morning preparation for school included listening to the WELC radio station with Sam Sidote. He was like a member of the family as he played music and gave news information from his studio. He would recognize birthdays and then draw a name of a listener as a winner of the birthday cake from Rucci's Pastry. I was a recipient on one occasion. We had to go to Welch to the pastry shop and pick up my cake. That was a special moment in time for me. Before we had television, we could listen to children's stories, such as Looney Tunes or the Lone Ranger on radio.

I enjoyed my school days and socializing with other students. And I never received a marriage proposal until I was in fourth grade. One day, Billy Ray walked up to me and said, "will you marry me?" I was taken aback and told him I would ask my Momma if I could. I couldn't wait to get home and ask Momma if I could marry him. Well, she laughed out loud, "Oh, honey! You're way too young to get married." "Well, I said, I'll just ask Momaw, then." I don't suppose I pursued it because that is the extent of what I recall about the occasion. And I didn't hear anything else from Billy Ray. I suppose he moved on to other crushes and eventually found happiness.

Our elementary school took us through eighth grade at Superior-Maitland and we rode the bus to Welch for our high school years. A teacher at Maitland called Momma and asked if she could give my sister some clothes. Of course, Momma said yes. When I think of that time, I am touched by the thoughtfulness that was shown.

We traveled a winding path through the wooded hillside and down sloping areas before crossing a footbridge at the end of the main camp. Sometimes I stopped at my girlfriend, Wanda's house and waited for her so we could walk to school together. On a different note, a school classmate of ours whom I met at a reunion, recalled to me a time when she walked to school with my sister Alma, and me. According to her recollection, she said we dared her to rub a leaf of poison oak on her because she said she could not get a rash from it. Well, she took the dare and rubbed the leaf all over her face and arms and was a mess the next day, her eyes swelled shut, and her arms broke out. Of course, I did not remember the incident, nor an apology. So, after all these years, herein is a public apology for the incident that caused you extreme misery, Marg.

  I reminisce of my days at Superior-Maitland Elementary school with fondest memories. And when I remember our cafeteria which was downstairs of the school, I think of Sally Wilson, our cook. She prepared the most delicious lunch meals and made rolls that would melt in your mouth. She made cloverleaf rolls for the teachers' trays. I admired her skills, even as a young girl. Hot dogs and vegetable soup were served on Wednesday and potato soup with peanut butter and dill pickle sandwiches were served on Friday. School lunches were twenty-five cents at that time. We sometimes took a bag lunch to school. And I recall that sometimes we would trade sandwiches.

  I can smell the waxy scent of Crayola crayons and the chalk dust on the blackboard tray where the felt erasers nested. The wooden plank floors appeared to have grease spots on them, and I remember our custodian, would sprinkle something that looked like sawdust on the hall floors and sweep it away with a wide broom. His quarters, which we could see when the door was ajar, were in the basement of the school building where a gigantic, coal-fired furnace with metallic tentacles was fueled to warm our classrooms. As we played outside during recess, our childish curiosity gave us opportunity to sneak a peek inside the basement door, simply because it was off limits to children.

Our playground equipment was not only fun, but gave us beneficial exercise, as well. We had climbing bars, hand swings and see-saws. During our break we could purchase candy from a glass front case, which was opened during lunch and recess. If we were fortunate enough to have a couple of pennies or a nickel or dime, we could buy things like Mary Janes, a type of the peanut butter kisses, Black Jacks (the pink and black licorice) or sticky Squirrel Nut Zippers. If we had a nickel to spend at school, my favorite was the flat, caramel Sugar Daddy on a stick, which lasted much longer than a penny piece of candy.

During my elementary school years, Momma painstakingly sculpted my black hair into a massive bundle of banana curls, using Carnation milk from the can. Then she trimmed a straight row of bangs across my forehead. Just one flip of a curl from a little boy in the desk behind me was grounds for romance!

Fad and fashion prevailed even in my youthful days. The black and white saddle oxfords, which were in vogue, had more appeal to me than the black sandals I wore. So, I remember trading shoes with a classmate in third grade and when the bell rang to go home, we started out the building in each other's shoes and had to go back in and exchange them. Little boys, influenced by their hero, Davy Crockett, king of the wild frontier, donned coonskin hats.

In the fall we presented holiday programs on the stage of the auditorium. I clearly remember dancing to "Turkey in the Straw" and singing "Over the River and Through the Woods to Grandmother's House," as we looked forward to Thanksgiving and Christmas. Our school presented a fall festival each year at Halloween. Two major events that drew the community were a cake walk which required individuals to listen for the musical prompt, walk around the chairs and sit down before the music ended. The person who remained at the end received the cake. And bobbing for apples required participants to put hands behind their backs and put their face in a tub of water and grab an apple with their teeth. These were times of challenging fun. I don't recall lots of other events, but this was a much-anticipated event by the community, grownups, and children alike. Trick or treaters made their way through the community and kids sought out those folks who gave away nickel candy bars, which were given by the folks who were considered the 'well to do" and could afford them. A childhood friend of mine was talking about the Halloween experience and said that one lady in the community who handed out those candy bars would have the visitors take their mask down when they arrived to be sure it wasn't the same one over and over. A clever approach to giving out candy.

Seasons Change, winter arrives, and we find ourselves shivering from head to toe as the house warms while we get ready for our school day. Momma made cocoa for us in winter to drink before we went to school. Walking the long path through the snow and in winter's chill required some warmth as we set out on our way.

It is so hard to pull myself away from that Warm Morning heater in the living room as I make my way to the door. Getting up early this cold and brisk winter morning and traveling the rugged path to school presents its own challenges. The chill of the mountain air turns our words to a frosted conversation. "The hillside is steep and uneven; it can be very tiring to navigate. Bobby socks are a must and still my toes feel frozen by the time we arrive in the classroom to cozy up to the radiator " My brown paper lunch bag rests atop my books. My sandwich of sliced Treet with mustard will likely be frozen by the time I get to school or at least, I think it might.

We continued the winding path through the wooded hillside and down sloping areas before crossing a footbridge at the end of the main camp. The bridge led to a concrete tunnel under the highway, which exited on the school grounds. Sometimes in cold, snowy weather, going back home in the afternoon we walked through the main part of the camp because it was much easier to walk through the snow down in the camp than trudge through the drifts on the hillside.

Spring finally arrives! And in the spring, we celebrated May Day Festivities at school. We participated in the traditional May Pole dance outdoors where colorful, satin ribbons were woven into a work of art as we performed a rhythmic, "step-hop, step-hop" dance, to Miss McCoy's piano melody. She worked tirelessly to bring perfection to the festive event every year. Conducting the arrangement of every grade's performance for the great crowds of residents from Maitland and Superior. And the playground was graced with beautiful color from the decorations and the students dressed in formal fashion of white dresses and handsome suits.

In the spring, we were involved with the annual spelling bee. After we left the competition, our teacher took us to a small, locally owned diner in Welch for lunch. And when we finished our lunch, she said, "well school is about over for the year, so I'm going to go ahead and smoke in your presence." Teachers were not allowed to smoke in front of students during my school days and we were all surprised to learn that she smoked.

One of my elementary teachers had a book reading contest and the student with the most books read would win fifty cents. Before I went home this particular day, she spoke quietly to me and said, 'if you take a book home and read it tonight, you can win the prize this time. So, I did. Looking back, I realize that my teacher wanted to encourage me to keep my interest up in books. I was so thankful that day.

Out of gratitude and in honor of all those who influenced my life of learning, I applaud the competency of all my elementary school teachers. Notably, they were women of excellence and great role models. And they exhibited genuine pride in their vocation. They very much deserved the respect with which we were commanded to treat them.

The Girl Scouts organization was the only one that I joined outside of school activities. I enjoyed the challenge of earning badges that could be sown on our sash. Learning to make kitchen potholders was one of my first projects which was in the badge requirements. I recall that one of our meetings was held at the house of a mining company executive, because his daughter was in the troop. I was so smitten by the beauty and the size of the house. We walked a curved, hardwood hallway, past a tall set of windows over a window seat that led us to a spacious living room with fine furnishings. One of the most memorable events of my Girl Scout experience was when we were chosen to serve tables at a campaign, fund raising dinner at Brown's Creek Elementary School in Welch. The keynote speaker was Lyndon Baines Johnson who was John F. Kennedy's running mate for the 1960 campaign. I do not remember the details of his speech because we were moving in and out of the room to provide for the dinner guests. But his one expression of profanity surprised me because it was not allowed in our home.

I reflect on the fact that Momma gladly bought me a Girl Scout uniform and provided the dues, and there were the special school events that required costumes. How blessed I was when I look back and realize that a sacrifice was made many times for us.

Time passed and we found ourselves in high school and in a totally different experience. We were growing up. Subjects being taught meant that we would be changing classes and room locations. And we girls were not allowed to wear pants to school. In wintertime we were allowed to wear jeans under our skirt to keep our legs warm enroute to school, but once there, we had to remove them and put them in our locker and when school dismissed, we put them back on. We had to declare our diploma type and then we were assigned the subjects required. We would now be with other classmates from other elementary schools. It was a great thing to be making new friends. Some students would walk down the hill to the Tic Toc Grill and have lunch with others. Now, as we shopped in Welch, we could meet up with classmates and hang out together. And there was a city operated swimming pool that everyone enjoyed. And the prospect of having a steady boyfriend became another matter. We were in high school now and those sweetheart crushes in grade school began to blossom into romantic sentiments. The football and basketball teams, the band, and the cheerleading squads formed friendships as they met together often for their practices. In those days, couples decided if they wanted to go steady in their romance. The guys offered their class ring or a letterman jacket to his girl as a promise of devotion. Social life in high school was nurtured in the auditorium during lunch, or while walking to school or riding the bus. The local radio station would take requests for songs of dedication to a boy or girl and we all waited to hear 'our' song played on the radio.

When the transistor radios became popular, beginning in 1954, teenagers began to add them to their Christmas or birthday wish list. They were quite easy to handle and could be taken to bed at night to tune in to skip radio stations in Chicago, Fort Wayne, and Nashville. Romance was in the air and we could close the door to our rooms and listen to the sounds of Doo Wop at any time. My boyfriend owned one which was in a leather case and his favorite station, as was mine, was WLS in Chicago, and the legendary deejay, Dick Biandi.

Since my boyfriend attended a different school, our conversations were shared by telephone throughout the week and then in person on weekends. In fact, I met my boyfriend on the telephone. This is the story:

As he, from his house in Gary, was calling the radio station in Welch to request a song to be played, I too was calling the station to request a song. At the same time. When the operator connected me to the station's number, it sounded as if hundreds of people were talking at once. Then I heard a singular voice rise above all the others, "what is your name?" And I said, "what is your name?" He said, 'Give me your number and I will call you back." And he did! For the next four years. He was two years ahead of me in school so when I was a sophomore, he invited me to his senior dance which was held at a country club nearby and was an all-night event.

    And I needed a special dress for a very special occasion. So, Momma put a dress on lay-away for me… it was a gorgeous, yellow Taffeta overlay with Chiffon, yellow silk bows on the thin shoulder straps, and crinoline underneath. When I think back on that dress and realize that it was likely a sacrifice to purchase at twenty-five dollars, I am so humbled. I learned to never take for granted anything that was done for me. Then came the date of the dance and my boyfriend picked me up and we stopped at his house in Gary on the way to the country club and his mother let me use a set of good quality rhinestone jewelry, necklace, bracelet, and earrings. This was a grand moment for me…the bling, the dress, and the salon hairstyle. So special was the occasion, I felt as if I had been invited to a regal coronation. There was a dinner and dance for the seniors and doo-wop music filled the room. It was a memorable event for all of us. When we arrived home in the wee hours of morning, Momma and Daddy were up, in the kitchen firing up the coal stove for breakfast. The dance brought the seniors to the end of their high school career. Some seniors entered college, and many left the area for larger cities and new opportunities for employment in government and in factories. And then, some remained at home, as my boyfriend did and found employment nearby.

    Another notable event when I was a sophomore. I was given an opportunity to be a deejay for an afternoon at the local radio station, WOVE. After school, I walked to the building where the station was housed and enjoyed playing the music and talking between records. It was just the one occasion. Nevertheless, it was a unique and memorable experience for me as a young girl. We enjoyed an occasional movie at the Pocahontas Theater in Welch. Television programming began to improve, offering more variety of entertainment. Saturday afternoon westerns were my favorite! With added channels, we were entertained by comedians and musicians. The Lawrence Welk Show came on every Saturday night and our family enjoyed his style of music. We also looked forward to American Bandstand with Dick Clark. He had regulars who attended his show and became dance partners. Sometimes he presented an artist to sing on the show adding to the excitement. Doo-wop music and rock and roll dancing surrounded us on weekends and filled our summer with many occasions to go dancing which included sock hops and street dances.

I was in my senior year, sitting in social studies class when our principal's voice came across the public address system with a bone chilling announcement, "President Kennedy has just been shot!" And he repeated it, classes were dismissed, and students began to file out of class. I noticed several girls crying. I was eager to get home and watch the news to see what had happened. It was a sad day in history for us.

The Author

First Grade

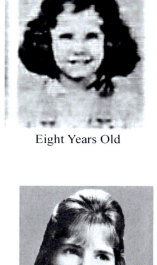

Eight Years Old

My boyfriend and me
ca. 1962

11th grade

Going to husband's
graduation, senior
dance, 1962

Superior-Maitland
May Day Festival

May Festival
attended by
Maitland
and Superior
Famililes

Superior-Maitland Elementary
School

There was a prince
and a princess, and a
king and a queen...

Down the mountain, across the railroad tracks to the foot bridge

The path from our house to S-M school

Steps leading to the front door of S-M Elementary School

Pop Beads

LBJ fundraiser dinner. My Girl Scout troop helped...

Watching for Momaw and Popaw

My childhood involved extended family with regular visits from Momaw and Popaw, aunts, uncles, and cousins galore. The location of our house on the hill afforded us an excellent panoramic view of the camp, the creek, and the railroad. We took vigil in the old metal swing on our front porch in gleeful anticipation of a visit from our Popaw. He relied on public transportation. The Greyhound bus he rode stopped on the side of Route 52 where we watched as he stepped outside the bus. We could time his arrival accurately as we watched him make his way through the camp, across the railroad tracks and finally, climb the hill to our house. Popaw's visits were not accompanied by lots of other family. Occasionally, he came alone. Momaw came with him when someone could drive them to our house. We just simply enjoyed their presence, especially at the table for Momma's home cooking. Momaw was never one to sit still for very long. She was always wanting to help Momma with any of her domestic chores. I recall that one time we owned a Chicken which was for the purpose of providing food. Momaw knew exactly how to process the chicken and we kids watched as she began. Wringing the neck was the first step, then she threw a washtub over it. She had boiling water on the stove to pour over the chicken so that she could pluck the feathers to a clean finish. And then, like a professional, she cut and fried each section. There were no fast-food restaurants for burgers or Chicken tenders, so folks raised their own chickens, hogs, and cows in open fields and on farms for their food supply.

When it was time for Momaw and Popaw to return home, Daddy drove them. We kids went along because, as Daddy put gas in the car, Popaw sent one of us in to buy ice creams like Brown Mule, chocolate covered bar or the ice cream cups with wooden spoons. What a treat!

Then there were occasions when kinfolks "overnight" visits were more boisterous.

Saturday Night: Kinfolks, Cement Fudge, and Burnt Popcorn Kernels

It wasn't necessary to dwell in a three bedrooms and two-bath house to accommodate all the relatives. Throwing around blankets and pillows, we camped out on the floor which served as a bed. We found joy in just sharing time together, sometimes gathering around the radio to listen to music from the Grand Ole Opry or programs like the Lone Ranger or The Shadow. And quite frequently, we conjured up ghost stories hoping to bring spine-chilling suspense to our time together. Inevitably, there would be at least one cousin, usually the youngest and most gullible, left in a tearful, frightened state! And, of course when confronted by the grown-ups, all the kids shrugged their shoulders and gave a puzzled look, "not me!" and no one knew the reason for the crying! The frightened cousin mystery remained unsolved, and it is a secret stored somewhere in the mountains of our childhood home.

Occasionally, my Uncle Jack, a handsome man with thick, wavy black hair, who had the musical talent of one who could have starred on stage at the Ryman Auditorium in Nashville, brought his guitar and a harmonica that fitted around his neck, and played very entertaining music for us kids. The tempo of some of the choices would have us kids up doing an Irish jig with laughter erupting and hand clapping from the grown-ups, urging us on to continue. All the family enjoyed entertainment in one form or another, the old-time mountain music or the kids and their dance routines gave joy to last late into the night. What fun we had filling the mountains with music, dance, and laughter!

Weekend visits were usually highlighted with someone volunteering to make the Saturday night fudge and pop the popcorn, which was offered even with burnt kernels. Because we weren't equipped with a thermometer to test our candy making, we were never quite sure how it would turn out. The hilarious results could be anything from taffy to cement. And should one of the kids get overly eager for a taste of fudge and lick the spoon before it was cool enough, a burnt tongue was the consequence. And that called for a potato to be peeled and then Momma would scrape enough of the potato to hold on the tongue to cool it quickly. A first aid treatment that worked.

To create drama with cousins was more profound than a haunted house, and the art of making chocolate fudge to perfection and popping corn without burning the kernels never reached perfection but produced satisfaction.

Oh, the stories that are being kept beneath the green beauty of my mountain home.

Family ties were strong during our formative years. Momma and Daddy had siblings who always involved themselves in our lives along with lots of cousins on my Momma's side. I can remember aunts being there and if the time of day warranted, they would help with our bath times and, if we were preparing for church, they also helped Momma with the polishing of shoes and such. The black patent dress shoes I wore were sometimes rubbed with lard and polished to a sheen.

That was family life when I was a child and I loved the fact that cousins, aunts and uncles would visit often and sometimes stay for a meal with us.

Uncle Harman, who kept bees and stored honey was Daddy's brother. He would come to visit us and sometimes bringing honey with comb in it. He would sit down to a meal at Momma's insistence. When it came time for dessert, Momma would ask, "do you want a slice of pie?" If he said, "yes", she would ask him how big? And he would answer, "Oh, 'bout the size of a mule's ear." That was his answer every time and it brought a chuckle to us kids.

And then, there were those times that we had fun on road trips with an uncle or aunt. They would come to the house to pick us up for new travels.

One summer, my sister, Alma and I were invited by our Uncle Harman to go visit his family on a farm in Virginia. I remember sitting in the front seat of that old truck, eating peanuts from a box and drinking a five-cent bottle of pop; sometimes pouring the peanuts in the bottle and drinking around them until the finish, then eating the soaked peanuts. Funny, how our conversation is lost in memory, but the event remains indelibly etched. What grand times those were for us, the coal camp kids to go out and visit other parts of the world! I was always smitten with each new adventure, enjoying totally different landscapes along the way.

Uncle Harman Greeley Snow
at Big Four, WV

Summer Vacations

Most of our family vacations were time to travel out of state to visit Daddy's relatives in North Carolina. He had brothers and sisters there who were farmers. If our visits found them busy with harvesting and preserving vegetables or fruit, it was the time when women gathered on the back porch to help and enjoy each other's company.

I remember Daddy driving me to North Carolina so I could spend the weekend with Uncle Ernest and Aunt Pearl and the joyful, childhood memories that have stayed with me over the years. My sister, Alma was supposed to go with me, but she had been sick, yet she still begged to go. Momma bartered with her, offering to buy her a record player to stay home. I think that Momma had been so traumatized in the loss of two children that she worried over us deeply when we were sick. So, Alma had a new small, square record player and of all the records she had, Elvis Presley's song, Teddy Bear was her favorite.

The rough-hewn, log house Aunt Pearl and Uncle Ernest lived in at the time was the home place of all Daddy's family. In fact, my dad was born in the house, delivered by a local midwife.

I loved climbing the steep and narrow stairs to the loft where I would sleep. So rustic! I awoke in the morning to the sounds of bluegrass music on the local radio station and to the wonderful aroma of fried ham, biscuits, and gravy. And the delicious ice-cold milk was as fresh as yesterday's milking of the cows I visited in the pasture. Aunt Pearl let me try to milk a cow but, I was not successful in my effort. Besides having fresh milk, Aunt Pearl made homemade ice cream for an evening treat. I marveled at the activities of farm life. I followed Aunt Pearl along the path to a fence where she would feed a calf from a milk bucket. And I watched as Uncle Ernest lifted those huge milk cans on to the truck bed and then head down the very long driveway to set the cans out for the company who purchased the milk.

Uncle Ernest kept a fire going in the tobacco barn where layers of tobacco were suspended from the ceiling, and he cured hams with Hickory wood in the same place. The wonderful aroma surrounded me as I lingered down by the fence. The scent of hay and newly-mown grass added to the experience. The water well in their backyard was still in operation and I loved to drop the bucket in, watch it unravel the hemp rope until I heard the loud echoing splash as it hit the water. Then, I would slowly turn the handle and draw up the full bucket. An aluminum dipper for drinking was usually kept nearby and on hot, summer days, the water drawn from deep in the earth was cold and refreshing. Uncle Earnest would sit on the back porch as I meandered around the yard. He would tease me at times, brush my bangs aside and say, "get your hair out of my eyes, I can't see you." He had such a way of making kids smile or chuckle at his sayings.

On another occasion, I can recall Uncle Ernest coming to our house to pick me up and take me with him on a chicken selling trip around the crooked and steep terrain of War, Six, Cucumber and Caretta. The wooden crates shook and rumbled as his old pick-up truck coursed its way over those rugged West Virginia mountains that caused me to bounce in my seat. Every adventure was such a delight to us, and we cherished every moment with kinfolks.

One of Daddy's sisters and her husband, Aunt Etta and Uncle Ed, worked a large tobacco farm and on one of my summer visits, my cousins invited me to help bunch tobacco to be hung in the barn. I did help and in so doing, the front of my dress became splotched with tobacco resin. When it was time to go in for lunch, we sat down to a long table spread with what seemed an enormous amount of food to me. I know there were probably seven or eight cousins in the family and there were probably hired farm hands working that day who sat down to eat. In retrospect, I see the reasoning behind fixing meals in this manner. Hard work for Aunt Etta and Uncle Ed that began in the wee hours of the morning and continued through the day demanded extra calories. Farm workers depended on meals prepared from scratch unlike today's convenience of fast food and excessive between meal snacks.

At Aunt Ethel's house, breakfast time was a delightful experience! After a good night's sleep in her country house, we stepped into a warm kitchen to the wonderful aroma of home-canned sausage sizzling in the iron skillet, while the delicious smell of Luzianne coffee with chicory perked to perfection on the old wood stove. And the fried apples she served with her homemade biscuits were most delectable! After breakfast, Alma and I would go to the back porch where Aunt Ethel kept her straw hats on a nail and choose one to wear as we went walking down her road. Two barefooted girls in straw hats enjoying our summertime visit.

Aunt Ethel was a hardworking, snuff dipping woman who enjoyed an occasional drink of whiskey. She was widowed early in life, having one son to raise by herself. Arthur, who never married, smoked a pipe, I remember, and he was loyal to his mother. He was much older than I so I don't recall any more about him personally.

I remember visiting her when she was a caregiver for a gentleman who lived in the town of Mount Airy. It was a short walk around the corner from the big house to a service station. Imagine my joy when I could put a nickel in a machine to buy an ice-cold coke! And the bubble gum machine got my attention because when the handle was turned, either bubble gum or a small plastic toy came out. And I had a collection of those little toys which I put on a string and made a bracelet for myself.

We looked forward to and cherished those summertime visits, when on our return home, we might arrive with a skirt made of colorful print, feed sack material or a new perm in our hair, compliments of an aunt or a cousin. We were no sooner home, when our anticipation began for the next summer's visit of new adventures and opportunities that unleashed our childish imaginations. Farm life. It was Denim, bib overalls and a work shirt, and presented to me a beautiful picture that was indelibly etched in my memory as I returned to my home. The place where coal was mined, and miners often walked to work dressed in hard hats and wearing a battery pack on their belts for their cap lights, and the miner's familiar silver dinner bucket.

Coalwood

Uncle Jack and Aunt Helen

Momaw and Popaw's old house in Coalwood

Momaw and Popaw Baker. They moved to another county for retirement years.

Momaw Baker in front yard of her house in Coalwood

More Gems from a Childhood Treasury

While modern technology keeps shoving me forward in the name of progress, I must plant the stakes of childhood memories deeper into the earth of my childish spirit.

Like sunlight upon a diamond revealing a many-faceted jewel, so is the curiosity of a child when released to nature's elements on a summer day. My siblings and I spent many enchanted summer days and nights at our grandparent's house, locking away a treasure chest full of golden memory nuggets.

Our affectionate terms for our grandparents were "Momaw" and "Popaw." Planning a trip to their house was one of the most-looked-forward to events we ever experienced, due mostly to the fact that individual attention was given during our time with them. I feel extremely blessed to have known a set of my grandparents who were so full of wisdom and love and compassion.

Momaw and Popaw lived in one of the company houses in Coalwood and we were so pleased that they had an actual bathroom. We had to step out on the back porch to enter the door, though. But it was much better than going out a path in the dark. Popaw found Ginseng growing near his house and he dug the roots and hung it on the porch to dry. He used it medicinally, but I never did know how he prepared it.

Upon arrival at Momaw and Popaw's house, we were always greeted with loving hugs and kisses and that good, "old" smell to the house.

Then Popaw, supported by his wooden, homemade stick cane, would make his way to the room where a huge wardrobe stood, hiding our orange, marshmallow, circus peanut candy, the peanut butter kisses and the Fleer's Dubble Bubble gum which was wrapped in waxy paper with a fortune written on it. We opened the wrapper of that gum with mysterious anticipation of what we might learn about ourselves. But it was only good for a laugh!

If other cousins appeared on the same weekend of our visit, we competed for Popaw's attention because that meant extra candy. Popaw displayed such love for his grandkids! While perched upon his knee, I recall the lingering sweet, aromatic presence from the pouch of Beech Nut chewing tobacco he kept in his flannel shirt pocket. The passing of years had turned his hair a snowy white and wrinkled his thin, pale skin. His crystal blue eyes were magnified behind the thick lens glasses, which were the result of cataract surgery, long before the age of high-tech medicine.

And, oh, how Popaw loved to sing the old-time hymns! There seemed to be an ethereal longing in his raspy, halting voice as he sang *Amazing Grace* and *Precious Memories*. Once I was old enough to do so, he would have me read scriptures from the Bible to him. He had such love and reverence for God and His Word. I have heard Momma recall some of the proverbs my Popaw often quoted; and this one has remained with me through the years, "you can catch more flies with honey than vinegar." Though not given in those words, they contain scriptural relevance.

Popaw's philosophical approach to life showed up in the spring when he consulted his Rexall drugstore calendar for the proper times to plant his garden. I remember hearing references to planting in the "new of the moon" and not planting certain crops when the signs were in the feet. And potatoes had to be dug on a certain moon or they would not keep well.

Advertisements printed on those local drugstore calendars, included: Cardui tablets, Carter's little liver pills, SSS tonic, liniments and Musterole rub.

Popaw's planting always yielded an abundance of produce; from the raspberries and juicy, purple Concord grapes to the smooth-skinned, tender red and yellow tomatoes. He always planted a good crop of sweet corn on the cob, too. We feasted sumptuously on homegrown and home-canned foods.

Momaw was a woman of substance in stature, with long, white hair, which she always twisted on top of her head into a bun, fastened by old time hairpins. In her neighborhood, women in the pains of childbirth or sick with fever would call on her for help. True to her nature, she answered the call. Her bibbed apron, usually made of muslin, revealed a hard-working spirit evidenced by the permanent stains. A grandmother's apron is multi-purpose. I recall times when she would gather green beans in her apron, carry them in the house and begin to string them without emptying them into a container. She used to string green beans (like stringing popcorn) and hang them to dry so she could have "leather britches" in the winter. Her apron might be used to carry in a dozen or so ears of corn from the garden. And the apron always had pockets for extra safety pins or to carry clothespins for laundry that was done on the old Maytag, wringer washer.

Momaw was a good cook, too. The kitchen cabinet where she created her tasty breads, cakes and pies, had an enamel work surface and a pull-down, flour storage bin attached to a sifter. It seemed that breakfast was always a hearty offering. Often there were large numbers of people to feed at Momaw's house. She cooked home fried potatoes, chopped into small pieces. They had a unique flavor to them which, I learned in later years, was due to the sprinkling of sugar she added.

She would make a large skillet full of gravy and fried eggs and if cooking apples were in season, that was an extra treat, because they were great piled on biscuits. I don't remember apples being called by names like, Jonathan, Rome or Granny Smith...they were always cookin' apples. As we gathered around the table with voracious appetites, it was not only respectable but also mandatory to wait until Popaw said grace over the meal we were about to partake. But, at times his Sunday morning, sermon-type prayers seemed to bless the whole earth. On some occasions, he would open his eyes to discover the grandbaby perched on his lap had eaten his meal. As kids, we got to enjoy the best part of summer, the outdoors! Once the meals were over, we headed outside.

Except that my red-hair, freckle faced, sister, Alma and I had to take care of the dishes first. So, we headed into the kitchen and began washing and drying dishes. We were young, but responsibility and respect for our elders was being taught along with learning to be thankful. Our conversation drifted into a few moments of loud singing along with a hymn that came on the radio. We were introduced to the music of the church at an early age. I remember our laughter when we forgot some of the words to that song and we laughed so hard, she with dishtowel fanning the air, as I stood with hands in soapy dish water, laughing uncontrollably, leaning over the sink to brace myself. Oh, how I cherish those times together!

Once the kitchen was cleaned, we could go outdoors, sit in the swing on the front porch and enjoy watching the neighbors come and go. We always took a walk next door to our Uncle Howard's house while it was still daylight. There was a mountain stream that flowed through his property and the wild, orange Jewelweed blooms added to our experience of walking barefoot through the water. Sometimes there were a couple of cows grazing along the fence line.

After Popaw mowed the grass with the old clacking push mower, we loved to roll down the sloped yard until we got so dizzy, we couldn't stand up; never mind that newly-mown grass had a way of staining, not only your clothes, but your knees and elbows as well! Once the mowing was done, Popaw would bring out a huge, green, and white striped, oval watermelon and cut large wedges for us to eat. We would eat the melon into the white rind, savoring every morsel. That melon added so much enjoyment to our summertime activity.

There was a musty cellar behind the house where Momaw stored all the foods she had preserved. We were allowed only occasionally to go inside this "place," which in our childish fantasy, was a place of deep, dark mysteries. A single cord light fixture with a chain pull was suspended from the top of the structure and there were shelves and shelves of green, Ball or Mason jars with those gray lids and rubber rings for sealing. At our grandparent's house, there seemed to be endless opportunities for exploration to satisfy even the grandest imagination... And we waited excitedly on the porch swing as lightning bugs filled the darkness around us. Nighttime slowly filled in the sky above and we enjoyed a light show, unsurpassed in presentation for an audience of two. We could easily trace the flickering from the grass on the lawn to the branches in the trees. What joy was found in those moments, indelibly etched in our memories. And they had a front porch swing that would rival any amusement park ride. We would push so hard I was sure we would land on the roof at any time, but we did not. The wood-framed screen door that led out to the porch was the only one that was locked on hot summer nights. The main door was hardly ever closed, much less locked!

      No matter how many times we went, visits to the grandparents always contained an element of surprise and delight. I do not remember complaining about being bored. The excitement of spending time at Momaw's and Popaw's was rekindled each time you walked through the door greeted once again with welcoming hugs, kisses, and secretly hidden candy.

Church Goin'
and the Inception of Assembly of God Church

When I was a child, we attended the Assembly of God Church in Vivian, pictured here. The church continues today.

My Uncle, Early Snow, documented the history of this little church and we are so grateful for his recollections which are rich in memories. His account is as follows:

The church by the side of the road.

The prospective members began meeting in an old motor barn in Tidewater. Brother Roy Cook recommended this church to him, he states in his writing. The meetings were later moved to the Union and Safety House in Carswell in 1950 and this building is currently being used as the Kimball Light and Water Company's pump house.

Depending on an old coal stove for heat, the members moved into the unfinished church building at its present location. After moving in, final construction was begun in 1950 and completed in 1952. The men who helped in the finished work of the building were, Rev. John McPeak, Early Snow, Parlie Snow (Early's brother and my dad), Creed Goodson, Brother Rush (Rev. McPeak's brother-in-law), Wiley Sizemore, Tom Osborne, Bill Trump, Glen Donohue, Doc Gentry, Albert Phillips, and Frank Martin.

Uncle Early further notes: The foundation was graded out by gasoline shovel. The sleepers for the floor of the church were done by Tab Gentry and Ike Gentry assisted in placing the roof. Several large trucks were hired and brought to the site to haul dirt, which was transported to and dumped on the present location of Kimball Elementary School.

The framing for the building was contributed by Koppers Coal Company. Flooring and storm sheeting came from a firm in North Carolina. Uncle Early was responsible for cutting the framing and rafters on the floor and joining them together. Once they had additional help, they then raised the framing in sections. The parsonage was started in 1953, for which Tab Gentry laid the foundation. The church members purchased the old theater at Eckman and used lumber from that acquisition. Framing out of the 2x12's was cut with a power saw. Again, Uncle Early put the framing and rafters together, put them in place and started the sheeting. The mines at Maitland shut down and following that Uncle Early went to North Carolina. He notes that the church members brought the construction of the parsonage and the church to completion after he had moved from the area.

He does state that Reverend John McPeak, the preacher I remember, was the main builder of the church and parsonage and was the first pastor there, but he could not recall who completed the parsonage. Brother John and Sister Nellie were there for many years.

Sunday school, church, and home prayer meetings were common occurrences for us. All preparations for Sunday were made on Saturday night; shoes were shined, clothes made ready, and the car was fueled. We could not rely on Sunday stops for incidentals because businesses were not open.

However, I also remember going to Saturday evening church services. As we drove through Kimball, we sometimes made a stop at an old store to purchase a cookie or gum or mints. The sprawling, wooden store building counter had a glass front display case at the entrance. On top of that, were glass jars filled with goodies; everything from pickles and hot sausages to cookies. The large, vanilla cookies were an occasional treat for us as we rode back home from church. Daddy would sometimes buy little mouth fresheners called Sen-Sen. These were very tiny, black, licorice flavored squares packaged in an envelope.

Church services were an emotionally charged spiritual event, where I remember very warm welcomes by the congregation. Friendly, happy faces, and firm hugs always greeted you at the door with church members addressing each other as "Brother" or "Sister." The upbeat music was played on tambourines, accordions, guitars, and pianos. The service opened with the question, "any birthdays this week?" If there was anyone who celebrated a birthday, they would go to the front of the church and have their pennies ready to count and the whole congregation joined in. That money from birthdays was collected and used for missionary work. The ladies of the church had monthly meetings at members' houses. Momma told me she remembered them having a Lemon squeeze to see how many seeds were in the lemon and then each one would give a penny for every seed inside the lemon. A unique way to raise funds to distribute for needs that arose in the church or community.

After the opening services of church on Sunday morning, we would head to the basement rooms downstairs for Sunday School. Afterwards we went to the sanctuary for regular worship services.

The red-faced delivery of the preacher's sermons from the pulpit spoke of his devotion to the Sovereign God. Foot washings happened from time to time as part of the morning message, symbolizing the humility that Jesus taught and exemplified in the Bible. Baptizing took place in the creek, located in Bottom Creek Holler. And when folks got sick, the preacher was often called for instead of a doctor.

Traditionally, at Christmas time, the children attending Sunday School classes were given a treat bag which contained gumdrops, chocolate drops, an orange and apple and a few mixed nuts, as well as the old-fashioned, tasty hard candies. Since this was a time of scarcity for some, we looked forward with great anticipation for those treat bags at Christmas.

I am so thankful for the spiritual lessons we learned as children, growing up in the church environment with friends and neighbors who became like family. Sunday School and church services had a prominent place among the residents of each community.

Church picnics, and all-afternoon playing outdoors when the meal was finished and witnessing baptisms in the creek. Sunday was family time and appreciation for all of those in the fellowship who strengthened our faith.

Tribute to Momma

*Pond's Cold Cream, Vegetable Soup
and Applications of Love.*

    The clappy sound of her suede high heels hitting the pavement as we made our way to the beauty shop for my perm. We rode the bus into town for this trip. After my hair had undergone the transformation from straight to curly, we ventured on to the drugstore counter where Mom ordered our grilled cheese sandwiches and cherry smash to drink. Once we finished our brief lunch, I walked beside Momma, listening to the rhythmic clapping of her suede high heels as we hit the pavement, heading back to the bus terminal. The sound of those heels against the sidewalk pavement has been etched on my memory, evoking such a sentimental moment.

    As children, we don't realize the memories in the making; the preciousness of time with a mother or dad who are investing in us through our formative years.

    It's those sounds, like the clapping of a mother's heels on the sidewalk, the beautiful fragrance of her Pond's cold cream, and yes, on days when she is investing time and energy in producing clean clothes, we get a whiff of the Tide laundry detergent, the Fleecy White bleach or the little block of Satina she used in the starch to make smoother ironing--- the sounds, the fragrances, are what stir up the memories.

    In glancing back, I'm reminded that the most powerful presence of my Momma was her loving touch; the gentle touch especially when we were sick. She was quick to bring out the home remedies, like a big pot of her vegetable soup, or a drug store purchase of whatever was needed, sometimes it was Camphorated oil for croup or Vick's VapoRub. Little did we know or fully understand, that beneath the outstretched hands that applied the medicine, from deep within her soul, the mother's love was being transmitted across our lives and imparted into our spirit. Unsurpassed love. That's the fragrance that lingers but it is also mingled with the clapping sounds of high heels on the sidewalk that led me to a beauty salon and drug store counter for that delicious grilled cheese and Cherry smash. Thank you, Momma.

The Love Letter I Carry in My Heart

A cold January day it was as I drove away from Momma's house. I was there to discuss having a nurse to come for home health care. Little did I know when we drove away---. But this I knew; God had the perfect answer for her. And the answer came much too quickly. She died in the wee hours of the next morning. This woman whom I loved dearly, who lived unselfishly. Indelibly etched in my soul are the times when Momma was portraying the example of a strength and grace not known by all, but some.

My mother's role in our family influenced my development because she never discouraged me from trying to learn from her. She exemplified a woman with endurance to weather the storms of life. And the storms…oh, how they blew upon our family!

There was just something about my Momma's presence as well as her cooking over the years that has written on my heart a love letter that I am able to go back and read over and over…I believe it must have been a "mother's measure of love" that was added to every dish she prepared and every task that was to be completed.

She watches over the ways of her household and does not eat the bread of idleness. Her children rise and call her blessed; Prov. 31:28.New King James Version

Gardening was one of Momma's great passions and after she passed, I looked out her bedroom window to a piece of land that she would no longer be tending. Sadness and Nostalgia washed over me, carving out a deep imprint of her love and unselfishness.

WHERE ONCE A GARDEN GREW

Where once a garden grew, now stands green grass and briars
within the cold, damp sod.
Where once a garden grew,
Momma talked with God.
The soil lies not fallowed now, untouched
by Momma's precious hands.
But memories flood my mind,
while on this spot I stand.
I hear her voice echo when I visit,
"Come, look at the tomatoes and the corn
by the green bean vines!"
I remember how blessed she was and acknowledged,
    "by God's grace, this work is mine."
I cherish every memory of the good that she has done.
I am blessed to have had a mother who cared for
    and loved everyone.
Where once a garden grew, plants flourished
    in healthy bloom,
On this plot of land blessed by God, came fruit
    from the earth's dark womb.
Momma's love for God was seen--in the hard work and love,
As she tended her garden and watched it grow strong.
And at harvest, there came from her heart a song
    "I come to the garden alone."

The Moonlight of October

    I opened the door to the deck to see what this fall morning was serving up to see if it was suitable for outdoor sitting in my glider. A glance upward through the trees at the dark night sky, displayed the beautiful Moon hovering over the fields. I love the celestial scenes that present themselves so early in the morning.

    The Moon, It's brilliant light. So indelibly etched in my memory is a picture of an October evening after I had brought my Momma to stay with me as she recuperated from a hospitalization due to pneumonia in the middle of her battle with cancer. The Moon glowed brightly that evening as I stepped out of my car to go to the pharmacy and pick up a medication that my Momma needed. So brilliant were the stars in the night sky and the Moon took its place reflecting light from the sun. You see, the Moon doesn't have any light of its own…neither do we unless the Son's Light lives in us.

    The next morning, I wanted to do something extra special for my Momma since she spent her life always doing special things for us kids.

    "Momma, if you feel you can endure sitting up for the time it takes to shampoo your hair and then long enough for a home perm, I'll be glad to do it for you." "Yes, honey, I can do it." Momma always enjoyed a new "do".

My memories took me farther back; one year I drove to her house, an hour away, on her birthday because I wanted to take her to see a movie that she would relate to very closely because she knew the names of and was friend to most of the main characters in that movie and lived near them in Coalwood, where she and Daddy set up housekeeping. Oddly enough, October Sky was fitting as it is her birthday month. But I also wanted to take her for a salon experience of having a fresh hairdo. Then we went to lunch in the mall. We basked in the emotional/spiritual lift that day as we enjoyed our chicken sandwiches.

Back to the perm. I arranged everything to make her comfortable and using a large black garbage bag that I had cut down the sides, I draped it around her shoulders to keep her dry while I shampooed and gently massaged her hair. I had curlers and perm solution ready, so I began the curling and all the while asking her if she was comfy, well as much as anyone could be in her condition.

We made it through the process and my mother raved about the transformation her auburn hair had undergone. I knew that the hands-on time and Father's Spirit in me did His work. After getting her all gussied up as we like to say, her face radiated with a freshness that seemed to emerge from deep within, pushing past the reality of her medical condition, adding a smile that filled the whole room with notes of love and hope.

Momma took care of us kids, selflessly giving, never complaining as she provided us with clean clothes, meals that were prepared with heaping measures of her love. And, when I was small, the time she invested in creating banana curls in my dark hair or taking me to a salon for perms.

It was my turn to give my Momma the care she needed. She provided for us kids and now she deserved the royal treatment.

I looked out my kitchen window a couple of days ago and looked intently at the Dogwood tree just outside the front door. Just a few months ago, as spring was making its entry, I watched as the buds of that tree were transformed to a pure white bloom, vividly displaying a beauty that man cannot create. And then, I watched as my feather friends returned, like prospective homeowners on a real estate hunt. Some chose that Dogwood tree for the family they would reproduce. Those blooms were transformed to deep green leaves providing shelter for the birds. And now that tree is entering in to another phase but offering one more benefit to the birds of the air before going in to a winter's sleep. While the leaves are fading into shades of brown and softly falling around the sidewalk in front of the house, the berries are providing food for the birds that are still around and perhaps do not migrate. It's as if the tree is saying, "Let me do one more thing for you..."

And now, as I stand watching the display of nature's beauty, yes, including the fall event of dormancy, and rest from their labors, I see an analogy to human events and the changing seasons of growth. And it is a constant reminder to me of the One Who speaks through those seasons of life.

For that I am grateful.

Tribute to Daddy

I was thinking one morning about all the practical things that Daddy made to bring ease or comfort to our way of life. One picture that replayed in my memory was that of a rough lumber car port that daddy built on the property where we lived. He cut down some Locust trees in the mountains and they were hewn to fit the purpose because it is strong and reliable for support. The black coal dirt was the floor of that carport. The sparkle made the coal in the dirt recognizable. Our laundry room was the back porch and Daddy saw the need to install a plastic screening material around the banisters to keep out the cold winds when temperatures dropped.

Daddy was not an outwardly affectionate father. Our conversations were often aimed at getting work done around the house. When he brought in a truck load of coal, or finished chopping a pile of wood, he would say, 'you kids come out here and help stack this wood or help me shovel this coal off the truck."

And he reminded us when we went out in rainy weather or in the snow to put on our galoshes. These were rubber boots with metallic buckles that fastened them tightly against the weather. In warm weather rains, we would put them on over our bare feet and splash around in the rain and mud. Daddy was born at a time when people who lived on a farm learned to "make do" with what they had. We learned lessons by watching him put that in to practice as he dug out and constructed a cellar of cinder block and wood, where our home canned foods would be stored. One summer when I had finally worn a hole in my shoes, I watched as he placed those shoes on a piece of cardboard, traced the outline, and then cut an insole to keep dirt out of my shoes…needless to say, it was a dry weather fix.

And…

Daddy Carried a Dinner Bucket.

Daddy didn't wear a suit and tie to his job, nor carry a briefcase with important papers, either. In dressing for work,

Daddy wore the dark blue work clothes or coveralls and miner's boots. His fashion accessory was a cap light battery that attached to his belt and he carried a silver dinner bucket which toted homemade sandwiches, which were many times made from potted meat or bologna and a little snack cake thrown in. His metal, Thermos bottle was always filled with coffee. When Alma and I washed dishes, we debated over washing that thermos bottle because it had separate pieces to wash, and the lining was a glass material which needed to be handled carefully because we discovered it could be broken if dropped.

Momma kept up the house, the meals and tried to keep up with us kids; we, who roamed the mountainside filled with childhood adventure. And Daddy carried a dinner bucket from …

Our house. On the hillside. Built in front of the cliff that towered high above it. Our house. Four rooms and a path. May not sound exciting to some, but the property that it sat on offered many extras. Extras that included access to a huge mountain filled with adventure. Hillsides covered in summer with blackberries and Black Walnuts. And spacious room for gardening. We just had to make a clearing wherever we decided to plant it and it could be as large as one desired it to be.

Our house, our mountains, where every season offered new exhibits for a child's curiosity.

The call came on a December Monday.

"Your daddy is in the hospital and not doing well at all.' My stepmother's voice on the other end of the phone spoke with somber tone.

After questioning her and learning that I did not need to leave immediately, I set about planning to go to the hospital and spend time with him.

The recipe for applesauce cake that I wanted to bake and give him for Christmas, lay unused on the table. I had planned a visit with him after the holidays. As an afterthought, I remembered the gingerbread men I had baked and wrapped up several of those.

I arrived at Daddy's hospital room, grateful to have time with him. I asked him if he wanted one of the gingerbread men. Of course, he said yes.

I went to the nurse's desk to request a cup of coffee for him to enjoy with his home baked gingerbread men, for he told me he could eat one right then as he was waiting for his evening meal. Although his appetite had been waning, when he saw the food on his supper tray just delivered, he became ravenous. I arranged his food within easy reach, cutting the beef in small pieces, and buttered his roll and added milk to his coffee. He wanted to know if he had jelly on his plate and I told him no and convinced him the Jell-O would be an acceptable substitute. We made small talk, reminisced about his early days of work in the coal mines, and laughed as a spoon of Jell-O bounced off his plate and rolled down on to his bed covers.

When I felt it was time to leave so he could rest, I smoothed his bed and pinned his call button to his sheet keeping it within easy reach. Turning to go, I paused to offer a prayer for dad before I left committing his life into God's care and keeping through the night.

I called across the room as I left, "And, oh yeah, Daddy, Merry Christmas!"

"It's merry he said, but not Christmas." It was December 27th.

My phone rang around 3:30 the next morning. It was my stepmother. "A nurse just called to say your dad died during the night."

I was astounded! We had talked, he ate well and was in good spirits when I left him. I looked forward to another visit and felt hopeful that we would have more time together... time to gather fragments from the missing years and fill in the missing puzzle pieces.

Though deeply grieved by the news, I was also very thankful to have been with my Daddy on his last day on earth. We had a meaningful, heartfelt visit that evening.

Closing Remarks

About that little girl who fantasized and painted an imaginary future; as adulthood wrapped her in its grip, demanding more responsibility, with progress shoving her forward, she found herself with much more ease of work in the home as well as changes in the routine of daily responsibilities. And gender specific was no longer a factor in completing those tasks. As she turned a button instead of loading a bucket of coal in the cook stove for preheating the oven for biscuits, and pressed a button to set the automatic washer, when she tapped a small box on the wall to generate the warmth in her house and oh! the wonderful convenience of an indoor hallway that replaced the path that led from the back porch, what joy! What blessings to appreciate.

She was doing the right thing all along, wistfully occupying her "private fantasy" spot on the crab grass covered yard with shimmers of coal dust beneath her as she wove creative dreams that came true. Her involvement with close family members, over time, was nurturing within her a love of travel, a curiosity that took her away from the coalfields to the country life and in her dreams to distant places awaiting her arrival. Now she reflects on those moments and is so glad that she "brought something from home— her childhood home in the West Virginia mountains"

I married my sweetheart fifty-nine years ago. I graduated from high school in June of that year and we married in July. As I reflect on our family life, raising our son, Tim and daughter Teresa, I realize that I have brought something from home. The love of family, that now includes a son in-law, daughter in-law and granddaughter, Britni, strong work ethics, faith, and the ability to encourage others as well as our children, to pursue dreams, goals and healthy friendships as they journey through life. And over the years those dreams of distant travels have been fulfilled many times as our family has delighted in making memories together.   Memoirs by Phylenia S. French